W9-BLD-443

pretty little cozies

pretty little cozies

LARK BOOKS
A Division of Sterling Publishing Co., Inc.
New York / London

SENIOR EDITOR
Valerie Van Arsdale Shrader

EDITOR
Nathalie Mornu

ART DIRECTOR
Megan Kirby

ILLUSTRATIONS
Susan McBride

TEMPLATES
Orrin Lundgren

PHOTOGRAPHER
Stewart O'Shields

COVER DESIGNER
Carol Morse

Library of Congress Cataloging-in-Publication Data

Pretty little cozies. -- 1st ed.
p. cm.
Includes index.
ISBN 978-1-60059-376-5 (hc-plc with jacket : alk. paper)
1. Textile crafts. 2. Fancy work.
TT699.P74 2009
746--dc22
2008032657

10 9 8 7 6 5 4 3 2 1

First Edition

Published by Lark Books, A Division of
Sterling Publishing Co., Inc.
387 Park Avenue South, New York, NY 10016

Distributed in Canada by Sterling Publishing,
c/o Canadian Manda Group, 165 Dufferin Street
Toronto, Ontario, Canada M6K 3H6

Distributed in the United Kingdom by GMC Distribution Services,
Castle Place, 166 High Street, Lewes, East Sussex, England BN7 1XU

Distributed in Australia by Capricorn Link (Australia) Pty Ltd.,
P.O. Box 704, Windsor, NSW 2756 Australia

Every effort has been made to ensure that all the information in this book is accurate. However, due to differing conditions, tools, and individual skills, the publisher cannot be responsible for any injuries, losses, and other damages that may result from the use of the information in this book.

If you have questions or comments about this book, please contact:
Lark Books, 67 Broadway, Asheville, NC 28801, 828-253-0467

Manufactured in China

ISBN 13: 978-1-60059-376-5

For information about custom editions, special sales, and premium and corporate purchases, please contact the Sterling Special Sales Department at 800-805-5489 or specialsales@sterlingpub.com.

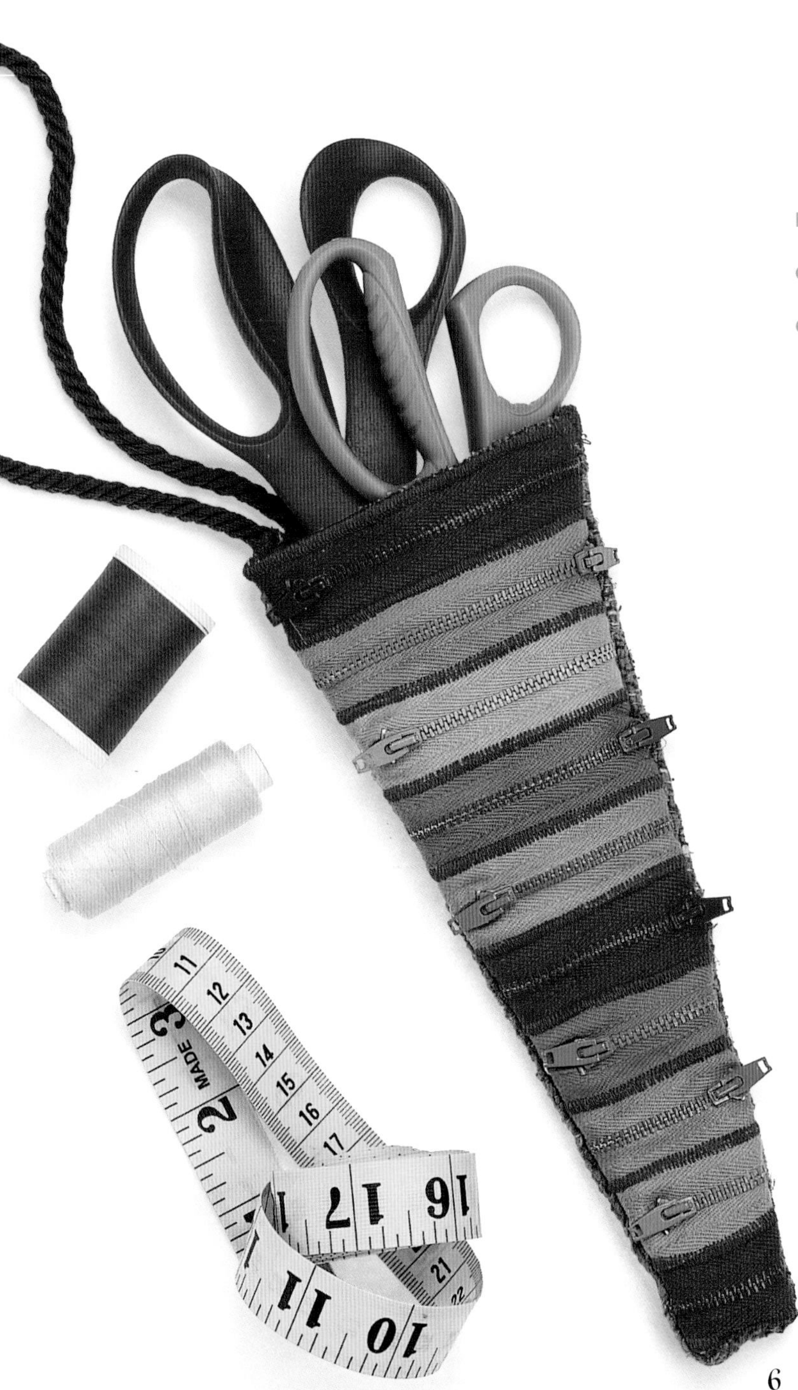

contents

Introduction

Cozies! They just make life, well, more snug and cozy. Custom cozies can transform anything from blah to hoorah; all it takes is some pretty fabric and a little bit of time. By adding your own special touch—your crafting stamp of approval—you can make something that is decorative *and* functional. Cozies can protect your precious belongings, keep coffee and food warm, and, most important of all, they're adorable little things.

When you make a cozy, you're customizing your environment. You're singling out your favorite objects and making them even more special. In the world of cozies, instead of nothing being sacred, everything is!

Once you see the beauty in the small things, you'll want to create beauty in *all* things.

At least that's what we discovered when we invited the most talented designers around to stitch up the most fabulous cozies imaginable. The result? Cozies that aren't just for teapots or beer cans. In this book, you'll find a collection of 32 cute little cozies made from gorgeous fabrics, both new and recycled. Every project brims with clever design and intriguing details and is bound to enhance your life.

Does your cell phone need a little love? Are your lipsticks feeling neglected? Do your art supplies need organizing? Find creative solutions to make cozies, snugs, and cuddles that work for you. Book Nook (page 47) exists just to keep your bedtime reading safe and sound. You'll love waking up to Egg Cap (page 108), a little house-shaped holder that snuggles your soft-boiled egg. Press On (page 115), a patchwork cozy for your French press, keeps your java piping hot. The Spectacular Case (page 50) is a must-have for storing your shades after driving to work. And in the backseat? Good Taste (page 94), a casserole cover-up to tote that tasty dish you whipped up for the company picnic. Since you'll want to take pictures of all the fun, keep your camera safe and sound in Picture Perfect (page 77) fashion.

So glance through the Basics section, where you'll find the low-down on materials, embellishment techniques, and basic construction methods. Then it's on to the projects, which are organized into three categories. Tech Head features all kinds of soft covers you can tuck your electronic gadgets into. Kitchen Stitchin' has cozies for food and drinks. And Cozy Life includes snugs for all those indispensible items you carry around with you every day.

What are you waiting for? Settle in with this book, set up your sewing machine, and get cozy!

cozy basics

It's time to get cozy with all the tools, materials, and techniques you'll need to make the projects in this book. If you're an experienced seamstress, consider these pages a refresher course. If you're a novice, use the information to master new skills. Either way, you'll want to refer to this section often when working on your projects.

A quick search around the house will yield many of the tools and materials you'll need to get started. Because cozies tend to be small, they provide a perfect way to use up your stash of scrap fabrics and trims. Keep in mind that cozies are great gifts, and by using what you have at hand, they're practically free for the making.

cozy tools

Root around in your sewing kit; you probably already own all the things you need to stitch up your cozies.

SEWING SCISSORS

Consider sharp scissors the queen bee of your sewing kit. Protect them properly, and they'll yield generations of great projects. Never use sewing scissors to cut paper—it will dull the blades and make them useless on fabric. If you're buying new scissors, invest in quality and comfort.

Think about adding a pair of fine-tipped sewing scissors to your kit. They come in handy when working on small projects, particularly when it's time to clip curves, snip ends, or trim detailed work.

CRAFT SCISSORS

These are the worker bees of any crafter's kit. They're the ones you'll reach for most often when cutting anything but fabric. Choose scissors that are a moderate length for ease of use on curves and corners. Use them when making your paper patterns and for cutting out templates.

PINKING SHEARS These shears cut a zigzag pattern that prevents fabric from fraying. Most often used to trim seams, pinking shears can add a decorative touch to any edge.

ROTARY CUTTER AND MAT

Rotary cutters work well when you need to cut through many layers of fabric, as for patchwork. But many crafters swear by them for all their fabric-cutting needs. Always cut the fabric on a self-sealing mat. Besides the standard blade that makes a straight cut, you can find pinking blades as well.

PROTECT YOUR PINKIES

Rotary cutters are fast and sharp. Get in the habit of cutting away from yourself, while keeping your fingertips out of harm's way. When you've finished cutting, always remember to engage the safety latch.

Basic Cozies Tool Kit

- *Sharp sewing scissors (for fabric)*
- *Craft scissors (for paper)*
- *Measuring tape*
- *Ruler*
- *Tailor's chalk or water-soluble fabric marker*
- *Straight pins*
- *Hand-sewing needles*
- *Thread*
- *Scrap paper (for patterns)*
- *Pencil with an eraser*
- *Iron*
- *Sewing machine*
- *Sewing machine needles*
- *Seam ripper*

SEWING MACHINE

All of these projects are made using a sewing machine. However, if you prefer—and have all the time in the world—you could hand sew many of the projects. When machine stitching, remember to follow a few basic rules. For thicker fabrics, choose a longer stitch and reduce the pressure on the foot, which allows the fabric to move easily through the feeder. Backstitch at the beginning and end of any seam that needs a good anchor. Use the zigzag stitch on edges to keep the fabric from fraying.

SEWING MACHINE NEEDLES

Nothing is more frustrating than finding you're out of needles. Machine needles are cheap, and it pays to purchase several packs at a time. Use them lavishly. Get in the habit of starting each project with a new needle.

HAND-SEWING NEEDLES

A variety pack of needles should take care of any general hand sewing you'll find in the projects. Some projects call for an embroidery needle. Its longer eye accommodates thicker embroidery floss.

KNOW YOUR NEEDLES

Don't be dull when it comes to needles. The most commonly used sewing machine needles are sharps, universals, and ballpoints. Woven fabrics do best when sewn with sharps. For knits, use a ballpoint needle—the smooth ball-shaped point prevents runs by pushing between the fibers rather than piercing them. Universals, not surprisingly, are good all-purpose needles.

NEEDLE THREADER

Keep missing the eye of the needle when threading? You're not alone. This little tool will save you time and frustration. Simply push the wire loop through the eye of the needle and insert the thread. Pull the loop out, and the thread follows.

SEAM RIPPER

Ah, if only life had a comparable tool for quickly undoing our mistakes. A seam ripper can get you out of any tight situations, putting you back on the straight and narrow in no time.

MEASURING TAPE AND TRANSPARENT RULER

A measuring tape is essential for any sewing project. Use a transparent ruler when you need to make a straight line or mark smaller measurements.

IRON

Versatile is not a word you often think of when it comes to irons—unless you're a crafter. Besides getting the wrinkles out of cotton and linen, use your iron to press seams and hems, and to apply fusible interfacing, transfers, and appliqués.

BORED BY BIG BOARDS?

Consider using a sleeve board for ironing when making small projects. You can set it up on your work surface in a jiffy. While you're at it, look for a mini iron. They get into tight and tiny spaces with ease, and are perfect when making bias tape or pressing short seams on cute cozies.

PINS

Purists tend to stick with the traditional short metal pins that have small heads. But if you like to show a little flair, use the longer ones with colored glass or plastic heads. Bonus—the larger heads make them far more visible, which comes in handy when it's time to remove them.

TAILOR'S CHALK AND FABRIC MARKING PENS

Reach for these when it's time to make your mark. The chalk leaves dust on the surface of the fibers. You'll find it's easy to brush the marks away once they've served their purpose. The ink in water-soluble fabric marking pens vanishes when the fabric is washed. It's always best to test the pen on a scrap of the fabric you're using. Certain fabric dyes may interact with the ink, making marks difficult to remove.

SETTING TOOLS

Some snaps, grommets, and decorative studs require the use of a special tool for attaching them to the fabric. You can purchase these tools wherever you buy your notions. Simply follow the manufacturer's instructions, and you'll be all set.

FAT QUARTERS

Love those little bundles of fabric you see in fabric stores? A fat quarter is a half-yard of fabric that has been cut in half to make a piece measuring 18 x 21 inches (45.7 x 53.3 cm). As far as size goes, they're perfect for making small cozies.

cozy materials

All the things you need to make cozies are readily available.

FABRICS

Playing with fabrics can be the best part of planning a project. But what fabrics are best for your cozy? It helps to know a bit about the pros and cons.

COTTON

Who can't cozy to cotton? Versatile, durable, and easy to sew, it's probably the best all-around fabric available. The different weights of cotton, from sheer gossamer to canvas, meet many needs—though medium-weight cotton is suitable for most of the cozies you'll make. Cotton comes in a virtually limitless selection of colors and patterns.

LINEN

Linen's durability makes it a great fabric for cozies that frequently travel in and out of purses, backpacks, and briefcases, like Undercover (page 38) or Bless You! (page 32). Though tough, its distinctive luster from flax fibers makes it beautiful. Linen comes in many wonderful colors and prints. Linen wrinkles, so iron it before, during, and after sewing to keep it smooth.

FELT

It's safe to say that felt is most likely a crafter's favorite fabric. It's soft, doesn't ravel, has no right or wrong side, and is available for purchase in just about any store that carries sewing or craft supplies. The squares or bolts of felt you find in stores are made from synthetic fibers. Traditionally, though, felt is made from wool. You can make it yourself from recycled wool garments. If you want to give it a try, look for the simple instructions on page 24.

CORDUROY

Corduroy is the hands-down favorite for those who love fabrics with pleasing textures. It's also cheap and durable. When pressing corduroy, you want to avoid crushing the nap. Place a thick towel on your ironing board for padding, and set your iron to a lower temperature than you'd normally use.

WOOL

Always a classic and classy fabric, soft, strong, and absorbent wool endures as a favorite for any project. Wool can be fuzzy or smooth, fleecy or ribbed, woven or knit.

DENIM

Who doesn't love their favorite pair of jeans? Rough, tough, and always in style, denim provides a durable fabric for well-used cozies, like Computer Snooze (page 60). This tight-twill cotton fabric most often leaves its signature in shades of blue.

VELVET AND VELVETEEN

Silk velvet is the epitome of luxury fabrics—with comparable cost. Unless you plan on using scraps that you have on hand from another project, synthetic velvets will work just fine. Technically, velveteen is made of cotton and has less sheen then its silk and synthetic cousins.

SUEDE

This tough leather with a soft touch works wonderfully for items you use and handle frequently. Swiss Cheese (page 36) is a prime example. You can seam leather by sewing it or by using fabric glue. When sewing leather, make sure you use a heavier needle made specifically for that purpose.

NASTY NOSH

If you're recycling wool fabric for your projects, be sure to clean it thoroughly before reuse. Old stains and perspiration can attract moths that love to lay eggs in the cozy wool fibers. Unfortunately, once the little larvae hatch, the fibers become their favorite snack.

FLEECE

Soft, fluffy, and warm, fleece adds a bit of lush, plush texture to any cozy. Easy to sew and durable, fleece is washable and quick drying. Fleece doesn't ravel, making it a time-saver if you want to skip hemming.

FAKE FUR

Never sew-sew, fake fur always makes a statement. This novelty fabric can add a touch of glamour or humor to your cozies. Any imaginable fur pattern is available—from zebra to leopard to mink—as well as colors not found in nature, such as bright pink, electric blue, or school-bus yellow.

CHENILLE

This fuzzy fabric's name seems utterly logical when you know *chenille* means caterpillar in French. The secret to chenille is the yarn from which it's woven. The fabric comes in many different weights, which are suitable for making anything from garments to upholstery.

OILCLOTH

Oilcloth is a waterproof fabric, originally made by applying layers of oil to canvas. Today the fabric is most likely a cotton-backed vinyl.

UPHOLSTERY AND HOME DECORATING FABRICS

Walk into a store specializing in upholstery and home decorating fabrics and you will see a wide array of textures, colors, and patterns in natural fibers, synthetics, and blends. The majority of these fabrics are medium- to heavyweight. Use them when you want a cozy with extra body or need a fabric with insulating properties. Practical considerations aside, use them just because they're beautiful!

FOUND, RECYCLED, OR VINTAGE FABRIC

This is one way to double your pleasure. Searching for vintage fabrics or figuring out how to creatively recycle that great old blouse is a joy in itself—then you get to make a cozy. So, how much fun can one person have?

THREAD

It's easy to become unwound when looking at the wide array of thread available in the shops. Choose a quality polyester thread for all-purpose machine and hand sewing and you can't go wrong. This thread creates strong seams, essential when slipping items in and out of their respective cozies.

FLOSS

Multi-strand embroidery floss in cotton, silk, or rayon can add the perfect decorative touch to your cozies. Taking time to embroider details can make your cozy truly unique.

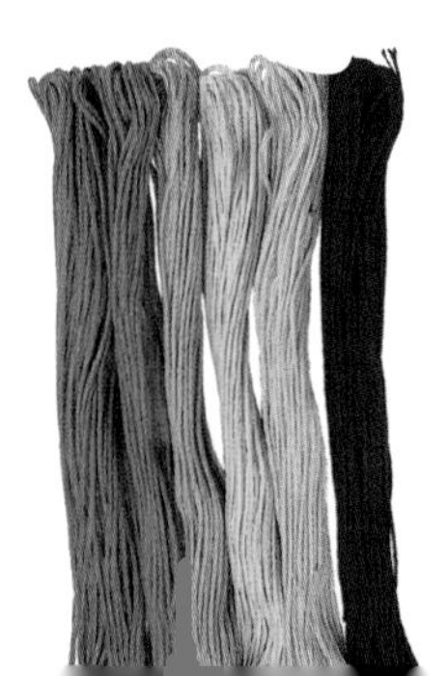

INTERFACING

No one wants a collapsed cozy. Interfacing adds any needed support and structure to help the cozies retain their original shape. Fusible interfacing, applied with an iron, is perfect for most fabrics. But never use it on velvet or corduroy because the iron will crush the nap. For these delicate fabrics, it's best to sew on non-woven interfacing.

FUSIBLE WEB

Fusible web, with its heat-activated adhesive, is a versatile no-sew alternative when you want to stick fabric to fabric. Paper-backed fusible web, much like double-sided tape, will adhere to two surfaces—just right for making and applying appliqués with ease.

BASTING GLUE

There are all kinds of basting glues available, in applicator bottles or glue sticks. Use these in lieu of stitching to add an embellishment or position an appliqué patch. With some vinyl or leather projects, glue can replace stitching altogether.

BIAS TAPE

Bias tape is made from strips of fabric cut on the bias (diagonal) rather than the straight of the grain. Its bias stretch lets it ease its way beautifully around curves and corners. It's essential for binding raw edges. You can purchase single-fold or double-fold bias tape in various widths and a wide range of colors. For a truly custom look, make your own bias tape following the instructions on page 21.

PIPING

Piping is a round trim sewn into the seam. Also called cording, piping is made by wrapping a bias strip around a cord, then stitching close to the cord to keep it in place. You can purchase packages of piping in a variety of diameters and colors.

FRAY RETARDANT

Found in both liquid and spray-on applications, this product binds with fibers to prevent unraveling. It's convenient for use on seams in tight spaces when you can't zigzag to overcast. It's also good for sealing the edges of appliqués.

HOOK-AND-LOOP TAPE

Hook-and-loop tape knows how to hold it together. Is this the best invention ever, or what? The tape comes in many widths. For even easier use, look for precut shapes, such as tabs and buttons.

POLYESTER FIBERFILL AND BATTING

Sometimes you just need to stuff it. These materials will add padding, insulation, or dimension to your cozy. Polyester fiberfill, which comes in bags, is convenient to use—just pull out what you need, stuff, and go. Batting, which comes in rolls, can be easily cut to shape.

embellishments

Adding embellishments turns something nice into something pretty.

RIBBON AND RICKRACK

Ends, bits, and snippets—few sewing baskets escape playing host to multiplying generations of leftover ribbon and other trims. These versatile and beautiful notions can trim, adorn, and tie.

BUTTONS

Beautiful, beautiful buttons; for some, collecting them is sheer addiction. Use them as closures for your cozies or let them stand alone as design elements. Use flat buttons when making cozies that travel. It will prevent the cozy from getting snagged or caught when removing it from your tote of choice.

SNAPS

Snaps are a most practical closure when making small items. You can use traditional black or silver sew-ons, or go for decorative snaps when you want extra embellishment.

GROMMETS

Tying down tents and tarps comes to mind when thinking of grommets. But these hard-working metal circles move from the edge to edgy when you think of them as design elements. Swiss Cheese on page 36 shows how to combine function and fashion beautifully.

EMBROIDERY

Hand-stitching on fabric went out of fashion for a while, but happily this pretty embellishment technique has made a huge comeback.

cozytechniques

Whether you've been sewing for decades or are making your first attempt, it all comes down to this. A quick review will get you sewing in no time.

MACHINE STITCHING

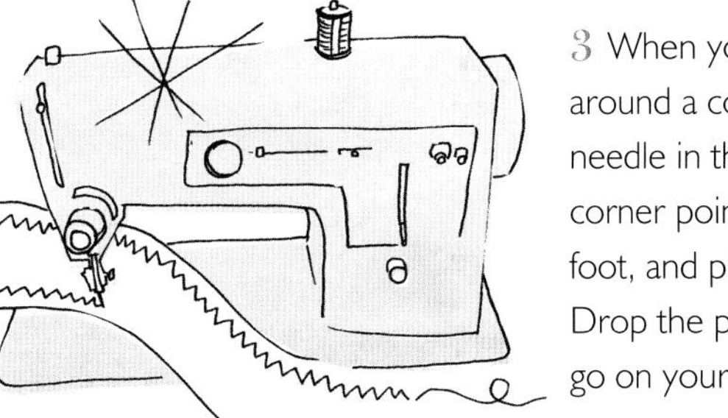

First, make sure your machine is set to the proper tension for the fabric you're using. Then make a test by stitching on a scrap of the same fabric. Look for stitches that are smooth on both sides. If necessary, follow your sewing machine's manual to adjust the tension for the top thread or the bobbin. Next, follow these steps for sewing the perfect seam.

1 Pin the fabric together with straight pins placed at right angles to the seam. Most seams are sewn with right sides together and raw edges aligned.

2 Sew the seam, pulling out the pins before they reach the needle. If you're not quick enough, the machine needle can nick the pins, which will make it dull. Worse, the pins can break the needle—and we all know how that feels.

3 When you need to stitch around a corner, keep the needle in the fabric at the corner point, lift the presser foot, and pivot the fabric. Drop the presser foot, and go on your way.

4 To avoid uneven stitches, stretched fabric, and puckered seams, let the machine do the work of pulling the fabric through as you sew.

BACKSTITCHING

To prevent seams from pulling apart under pressure, make it a habit to always backstitch at both the beginning and end of a seam. Backstitching involves nothing more than running the machine in reverse for a few stitches, then allowing it to go forward again for a few more. All it takes is a second, but it saves a lot of hassle.

Seam Standard

- *The standard seam allowance used for all projects is 1/2 inch (1.3 cm), unless the project instructions say otherwise.*

TOPSTITCHING

Topstitching is a line of stitching sewn on the right side of the fabric. It runs parallel to the edge or seam. Use it to keep a panel or lining in place, flatten a seam, or strictly for embellishment. Try topstitching with contrasting thread for added visual interest.

EDGESTITCHING

Edgestitching is exactly like topstitching with one small twist. When you edgestitch, you sew as close to the fabric edge as you can. It is less decorative and more functional than topstitching—it's one stitch that's happy to work invisibly on the sidelines.

CLIPPING CORNERS AND CURVES

Corners and curves look neat and tidy fresh off the sewing machine. The trouble comes when you turn them right side out. Excess fabric bunches in the seam, and you end up with less-than-smooth curves and lumpy corners. A few well-placed snips before turning the fabric will help you prevent this problem.

Corners—You can have crisp corners in one easy step. After sewing, simply cut the seam allowance at a 45° angle to the raw edge. Cut close to the stitching, but be careful; you don't want to cut the stitches (figure 1). When you turn the item right side out, use a thin, blunt object—such as a chopstick or the eraser end of a pencil—to gently push out and shape the corners.

figure 1

Curves—Clipping and notching curves ensures the fabric will lie smooth around a curve. You clip inward curves and notch outward curves after sewing. To clip, use scissors to cut into the seam allowance at several places around the curve (figure 2). Don't clip too close since you don't want to cut into the stitching. To notch, cut small v-shaped wedges from the seam allowance (figure 3), being careful to avoid cutting into the stitching.

figure 2

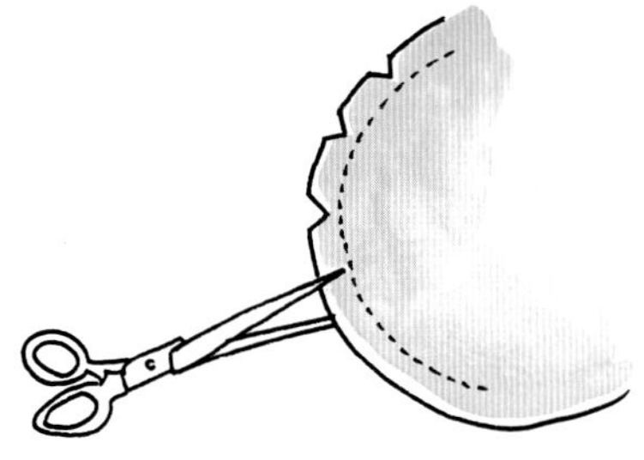

figure 3

ATTACHING BIAS TAPE

There are two methods for attaching bias tape, also called binding. If the binding goes around a project and meets at an end, as in You Rang? (page 71), follow the instructions for Binding a Circumference. If the binding does not join, as in Press On (page 115), follow the instructions for Binding an Edge.

BINDING AN EDGE

1 Measure the length of the edge you will bind; then add some extra for folding under the raw edges later. Cut this length of bias tape.

2 Open the folds of the bias tape and pin the raw edge of the binding to the raw edge of the fabric with right sides together. Fold both ends under and pin. Sew the layers together (figure 4).

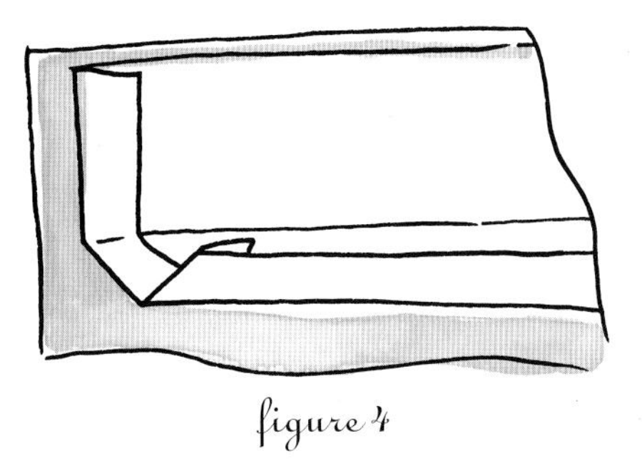

figure 4

3 Fold the binding over the seam edge, bringing it to the other side of the fabric, and pin.

4 Hand stitch to secure, or topstitch as close to the edge as possible, so the stitching hardly shows, making sure you catch the binding on the back (figure 5). (Because this may not look very neat, it's best to hand sew to obtain a clean stitch line.)

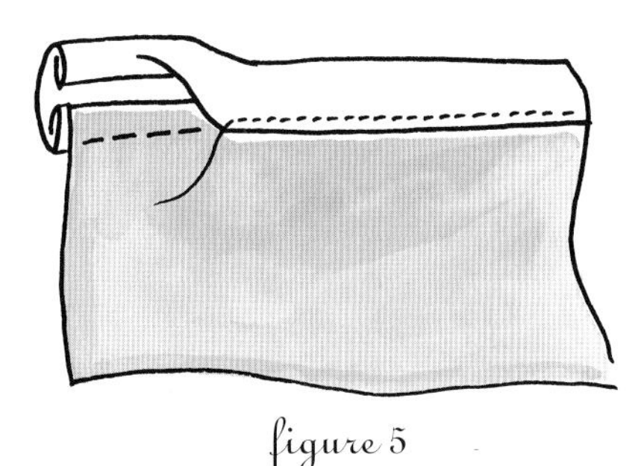

figure 5

BINDING A CIRCUMFERENCE

Follow the steps for Binding an Edge on page 21. At the end of step 2, stop stitching 3 inches (7.6 cm) from the beginning point. Trim the end of the binding to leave a 1-inch (2.5 cm) overlap. Fold the raw ends of the binding under ½ inch (1.3 cm). Continue steps 3 and 4, overlapping the end before finishing the stitching (figure 6).

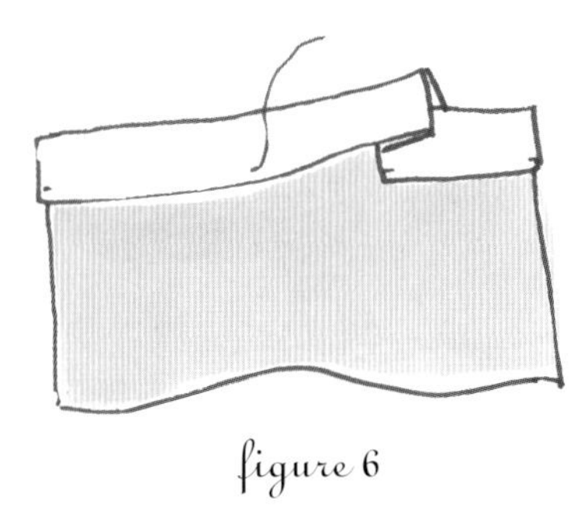

figure 6

MAKING BIAS TAPE

Guarantee a custom finish for your cozy. While purchased bias tape is convenient, you can get exactly what you want when you make it yourself.

1 Cut strips four times as wide as your desired tape at a 45° angle to the selvage (figure 7).

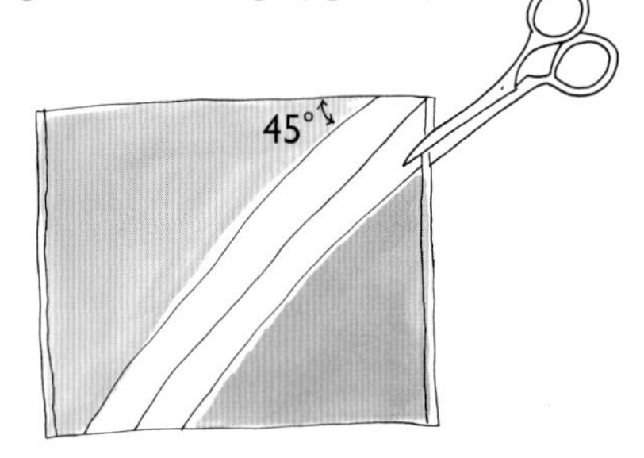

figure 7

2 To piece the strips, lay one strip over the other, right sides together, at a right angle. Pin, then stitch diagonally across the corners of the overlapping squares as shown (figure 8). Cut off the corners, leaving a ¼-inch (6 mm) seam allowance (figure 9).

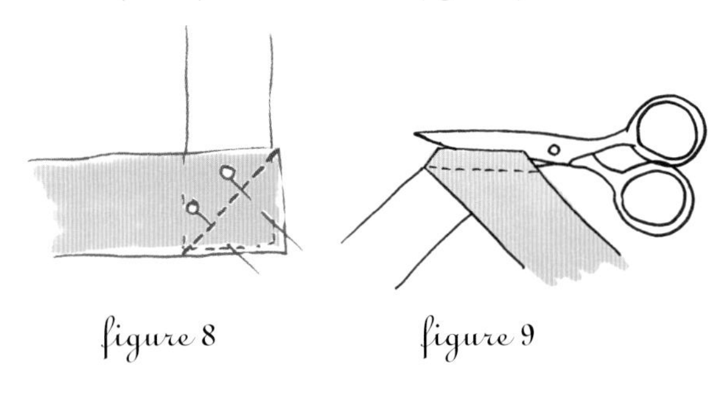

figure 8 figure 9

3 Open the seams and press flat. Fold the strip in half lengthwise with right sides out, and press. Open the strip and press the raw edges into the center. This makes single-fold bias tape (figure 10).

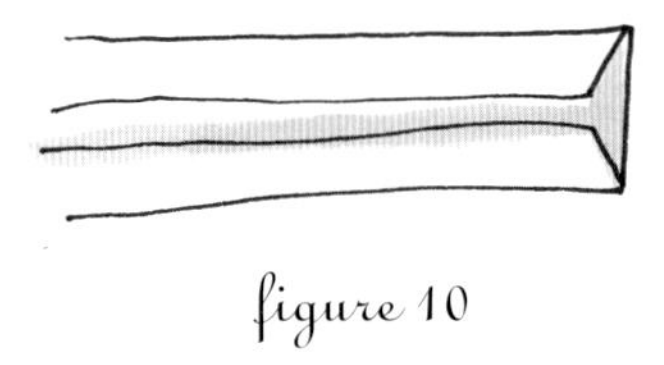

figure 10

4 For double-fold bias tape, fold the strip once again into the center and press (figure 11).

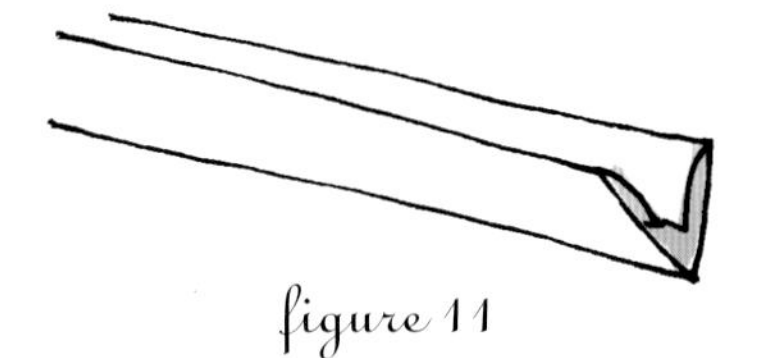

figure 11

MATCHMAKING TIME-SAVER

If you're sold on the look of bias tape that matches your fabric, consider adding a bias tape maker to your sewing kit. All you do is pass your fabric through this great little gadget (available in different widths) and press.

INSERTING LININGS

Whether you're inserting a lining to give your cozy a finished look, like the Teapot Cozy (page 97) and matching Egg Cap (page 108), or lining the cozy to protect it from wet and oily items, like the Spiffy SPF (page 52), it's easier than you think! All three projects use a simple slip-in lining.

1 Stitch the lining pieces with right sides together. Clip the corners, trim the seams, and press them open. Turn the lining right side out. Slip the lining into the cozy with wrong sides together.

2 If the lining is longer than the outer fabric, fold and press the edge of the lining under to make a narrow hem. Then fold the lining down to the outside of the cozy, as you would for binding, and then edgestitch or hand sew in place.

3 If the lining is shorter than the outer fabric, reverse the process in step 2. Fold the outer fabric as you did the lining, ending with the outer fabric inside, and then edgestitch or hand stitch it to the lining.

MAKING TIES AND STRAPS

Some cozies have tied closures, as on the Crafty Carrier (page 55), and some need a carrying strap, such as the Diaper Snug (page 44). Both are made the same way, starting with a strip of fabric.

1 Fold the strip in half lengthwise with wrong sides together and press, making a crease. Then fold each long edge into the center crease and press. The result should look just like figure 11.

2 Refold the center crease and press; then topstitch the long sides together (figure 12).

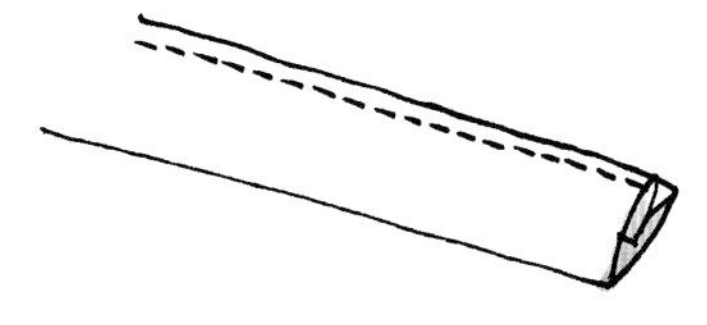

figure 12

SEWING A CASING

A casing acts as a tunnel for a drawstring. Basket Case (page 105) and Spiffy SPF (page 52) make their casings the same way. Simply press a narrow fold along the top edge of the fabric; then fold the fabric, wrong sides together, as if making a hem. Be sure to allow enough width to accommodate the drawstring you'll use. Finally, press the fold before machine stitching the casing close to the edge.

PIECING

If you want perfect patchwork, like Sew Clean (page 82), begin with two pieces of fabric and let it grow from there. Start by pinning the first two squares or rectangles, right sides together. Then stitch along the edge, using the desired seam allowance. Add more pieces in the same way to make a row. When one row is complete, make another; then pin and sew the rows together.

QUILTING

You can get a decorative, textured effect with quilting. It's also practical when you need a bit of insulation, like Press On (page 115), to keep your coffee hot. The quilting process is simple. You sandwich batting between two layers of fabric; then sew them together by stitching, either by hand or machine, through all layers.

FELTING WOOL

Using purchased felt is certainly convenient, but making wool felt is so much fun, and easy too! Use 100 percent wool garments—old sweaters are perfect. Make sure to remove zippers and buttons before you begin.

1 Set your washing machine to its hottest setting. Add detergent and toss in the garments to be felted. Let the machine run through its cycle. Toss in heavy items, such as jeans and towels, with the load to speed up the process.

2 When the cycle is done, check the fabric. It should be significantly smaller. If it isn't, keep washing until you can see the difference.

3 Hang the fabric to dry if you want a smooth felt, or throw it in the dryer for a rougher texture.

EMBELLISHING

These little touches bring a wealth of charm to your cozies. Whether you add embellishments before or after assembly, the bottom line of this equation is pure fun.

ATTACHING APPLIQUÉS

Appliqué is the fancy name for a decorative fabric cutout applied to the right side of the fabric. Using appliqués adds texture and extra visual interest to your design. One of the fastest ways to make and apply an appliqué is to use lightweight paper-backed fusible web (page 17).

1 Follow the manufacturer's instructions for applying the fusible web to the fabric. Do not remove the paper backing. Draw or trace the outline of the appliqué directly on the paper, and cut out.

2 Remove the backing and position the appliqué on your fabric. Press the appliqué with an iron, again following the manufacturer's instructions.

3 If needed, use a hand-stitched appliqué stitch (page 26) to keep the edges from raveling, or use a machine appliqué stitch. Another way to prevent raveling is to apply fray retardant (page 17) to the edges of the appliqué before affixing it to the fabric.

MAKING YO-YOS

Yo-yo is a nickname for gathered rosettes. These slightly puffy small circles are easy to make and add a playful texture to any embellished piece.

1 Decide the diameter measurement of the finished yo-yo. Measure twice that plus 1/2 inch (1.3 cm) and cut out a circle of that diameter.

2 Stitch a tiny 1/4-inch (6 mm) hem around the perimeter of the circle. It's best to fold as you sew rather than pressing the hem (figure 13).

figure 13

3 Gather the edges to the center by gently pulling one thread (figure 14). Secure the gathered center with a stitch or two, then knot and trim the thread. Don't press the yo-yo with an iron; rather use your hand to flatten.

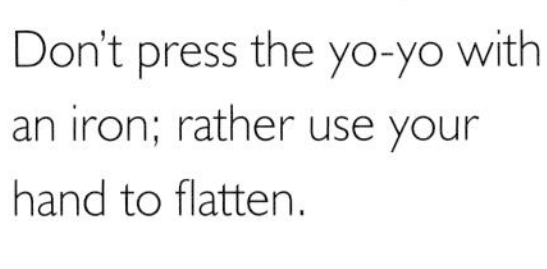

figure 14

APPLYING SNAPS AND GROMMETS

Sewn-on snaps can't be beat for pure practicality—a few stitches and they're secure. Decorative snaps are a design booster. Depending on the style, some decorative snaps can be attached using a hammer, while others need a special tool. Follow the manufacturer's instructions and you can't go wrong. If you place a bit of interfacing behind the fabric holding the snap, it will increase durability. Grommets also need a special tool for application; just follow the instructions for application. You'll be amazed how quickly they go on.

DESIGN AT YOUR FINGERTIPS

When thinking embellishment, don't forget your sewing machine's selection of decorative stitches. With a twist of a knob, you can add new direction to your design. Coffee Cup Quilt (page 110) shows how it's done.

HAND STITCHES

No matter how attached you are to your sewing machine, sometimes you have to pull yourself away and make some stitches by hand. Here are the most common stitches used for the projects in this book.

APPLIQUÉ STITCH

Use this stitch to hide the stitching that holds on an appliqué. Poke the needle through the base fabric and up through the appliqué. Bring the needle down into the base fabric just a bit away and repeat.

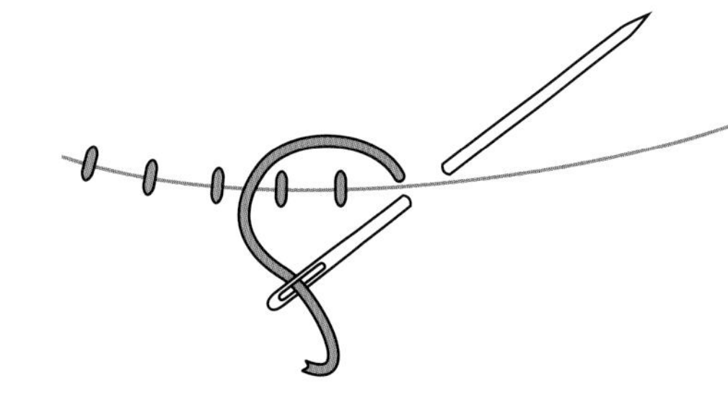

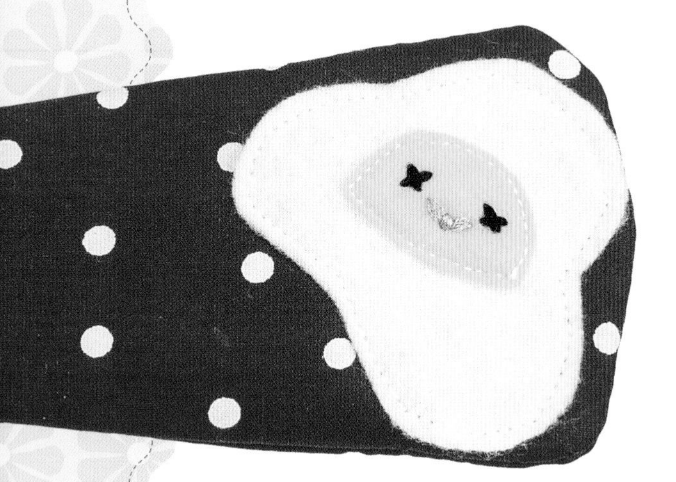

SLIPSTITCH

This stitch is perfect for closing seams. Slip the needle through one end of the open seam to anchor the thread; then take a small stitch through the fold and pull the needle through. In the other piece of fabric, insert the needle directly opposite the stitch you just made, and take a stitch through the fold. Repeat.

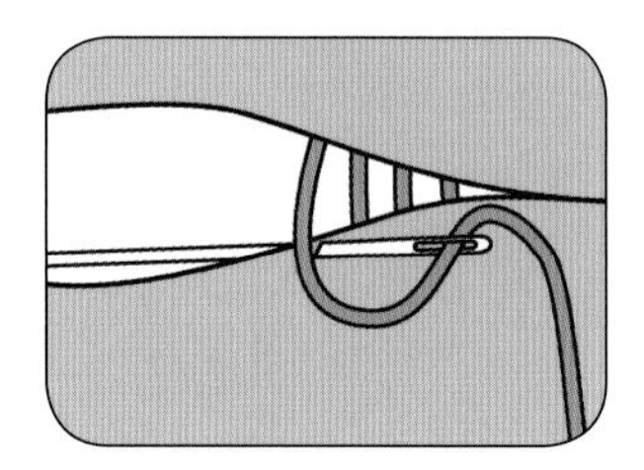

WHIPSTITCH

The whipstitch is used to bind two edges together. Sew the stitches over the edge of the fabric.

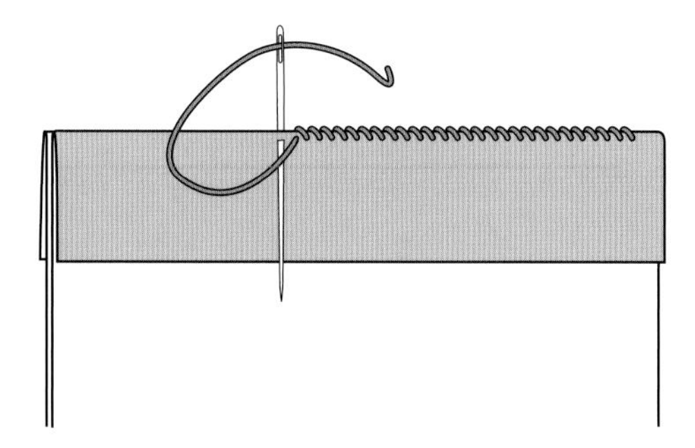

EMBROIDERY STITCHES

When you're ready to fancify your cozy with hand stitching, turn to these simple embroidery stitches.

BACKSTITCH

The backstitch can be used to create a seam or to outline shapes or text.

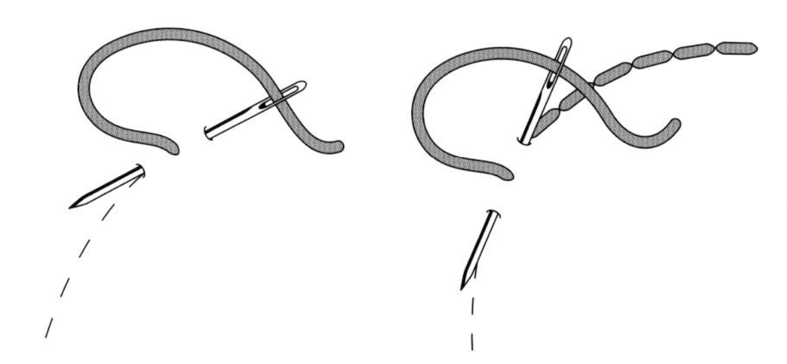

BLANKET STITCH

The blanket stitch is both decorative and functional. Use it to accentuate an edge or to attach an appliqué.

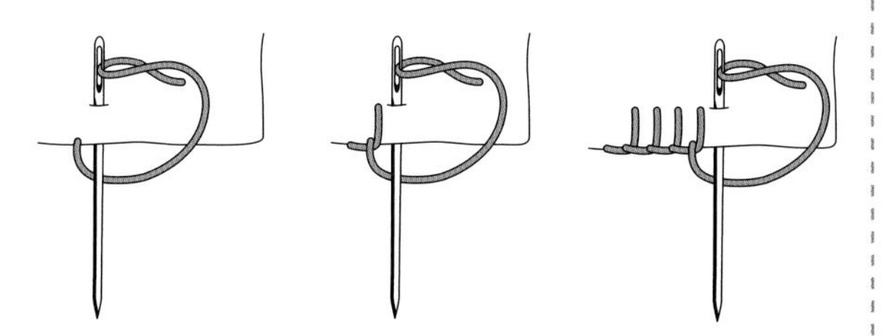

FRENCH KNOT

This elegant little knot adds interest and texture when embroidering or embellishing.

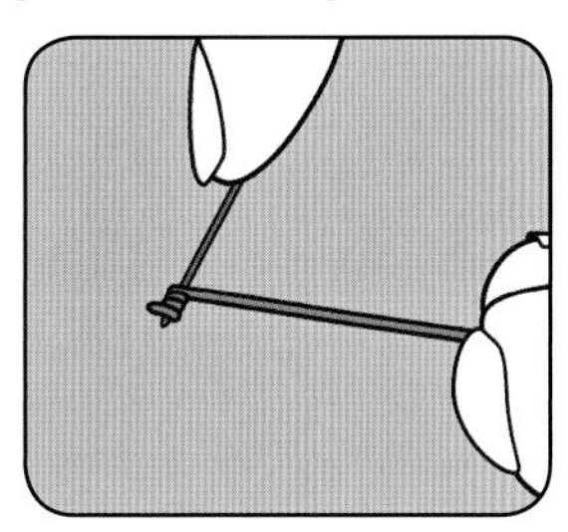

RUNNING STITCH

Make this stitch by weaving the needle through the fabric at evenly spaced intervals.

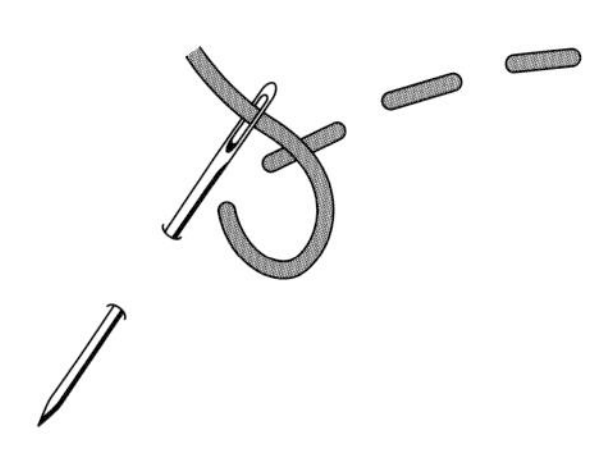

cozy life

From sunglasses to credit cards, keep your sundries snug in these spiffy cases.

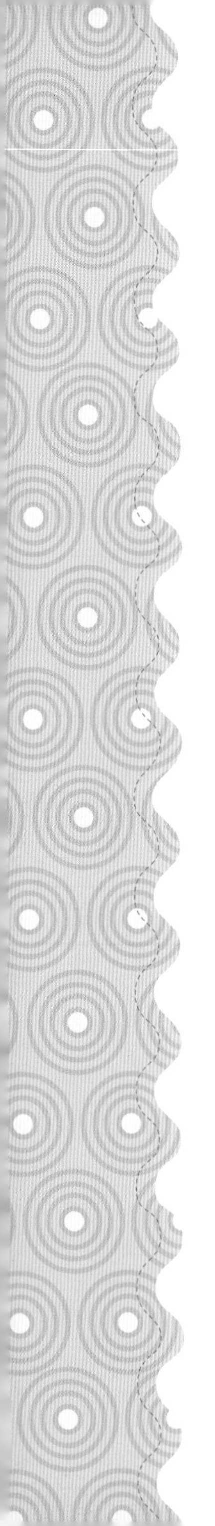

lipservice

Having trouble finding your fave lip color at the bottom of your bag? Make this case and kiss lost lipsticks bye-bye. With mouth-watering fabrics and a flirty button, you'll be pouting pretty in no time.

DESIGNER

STACEY MURRAY

WHAT YOU NEED

Basic Cozies Tool Kit (page 12)

6 x 18 inches (15.2 x 45.7 cm) of outer (velour) fabric

6 x 18 inches (15.2 x 45.7 cm) of lining fabric

Fusible lightweight interfacing

3 small snap fasteners

1 decorative button

WHAT YOU DO

1 Enlarge the templates on page 122. Cut one piece from the outer fabric and one from the lining. With tailor's chalk, transfer the markings shown on the templates onto the right side of the fabric. Also cut two pieces from the interfacing.

2 Following the manufacturer's instructions, fuse the interfacing to the wrong side of both fabrics. Pin the fused fabrics right sides together and stitch around the outside edge, leaving a 2-inch (5.1 cm) opening on the lower right on one side. Trim the corners and turn right side out through the opening. Tuck in the seam allowances at the opening and press flat.

3 Edgestitch across the short straight end, and then fold this end toward the lining to form the pocket that holds the lipsticks. Pin the sides of the pocket, and edgestitch from the bottom of one side of the cozy, around the top, and down the other side. This will secure the pocket and also close the opening used for turning the fabrics to the right side.

4 Hand sew snaps as indicated on the template, taking care to check the alignment before stitching and to stitch through only one layer of fabric. Hand sew the button to the outer fabric where indicated.

bless you!

Handle sniffles and sneezes with panache by keeping this refined tissue case handy. A satin ribbon and bejeweled button embellish the patchwork.

DESIGNER

RACHEL E. DOWD

WHAT YOU NEED

Basic Cozies Tool Kit (page 12)

5 coordinating fabric scraps

4 x 8-inch (10.2 x 20.3 cm) piece of linen

10 inches (25.4 cm) of satin ribbon

1 silver/crystal button with an "eye" or shank in the back

6 ½ x 8-inch (16.5 x 20.3 cm) piece of lining fabric

SEAM ALLOWANCE

¼ inch (6 mm) unless otherwise noted

WHAT YOU DO

1 Cut a 2 x 3-inch (5 x 7.6 cm) rectangle from each of the coordinating fabrics. Stitch them together on the 3-inch (7.6 cm) sides to create a strip of patchwork. Press the seams open.

2 With right sides together, align the long edge of the patchwork strip with the long edge of the linen piece and pin. Stitch the two together, and then press the seams up toward the patchwork.

3 On the right side, carefully pin the ribbon over the seam between the patchwork and the linen. Stitch as close as possible to the edge of the ribbon for the length of four patchwork fabrics. Stop and backstitch (page 27) just past the fifth fabric seam. Do the same on the other side of the ribbon.

4 Slip the crystal button onto the unstitched end of the ribbon, push it toward the stitched part of the ribbon, and secure the loose ends with a pin (figure 1).

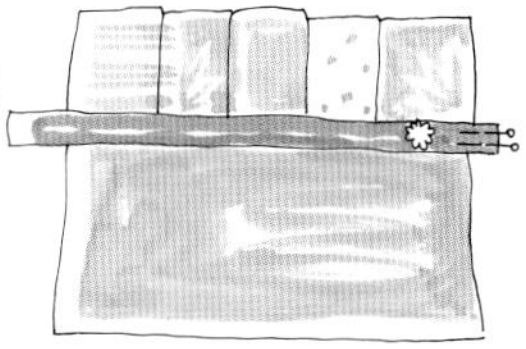

figure 1

5 With right sides together, pin the lining to the patchwork-linen piece. Start stitching about 2 inches (5 cm) away from the corner on one of the long sides, at the start. Stitch all the way around and stop about 2½ inches (6.4 cm) away from your starting point (figure 2).

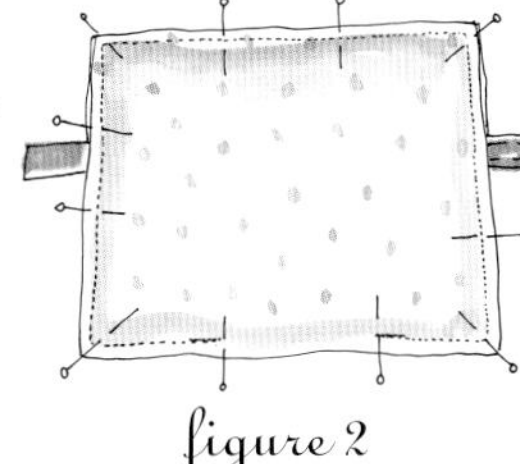

figure 2

KEEP IT COOL

Resist the urge to iron directly over the ribbon. The heat might cause it to warp or melt. Always press from the wrong side of the fabric or lay a scrap piece over the ribbon to protect it.

6 Trim off each of the four corners and the ends of the ribbon. Turn the piece right side out by pulling it through the hole left in the side. Carefully shape the corners and press everything flat—ribbon side facing down—with a hot iron.

7 Lay the piece flat with the ribbon side facing up. Fold over the side with the button about 2 inches (5 cm) and pin. Fold the other side the same amount (which will overlap the opposite side) and pin. All you will see at this point is the lining. Stitch the ends with a ⅛- inch (3 mm) seam (figure 3).

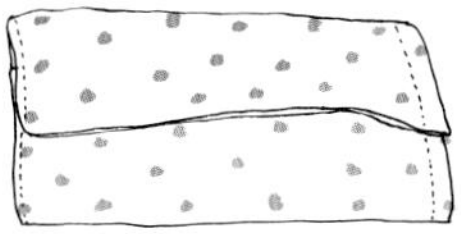

figure 3

8 Carefully trim off the very tips of each corner without cutting into the stitching. Turn the cozy right side out and fill it with a standard-size travel tissue packet.

cardcache

These days, who bothers with cash? All you really need when you leave the house is I.D., keys, and a debit card. This pretty little case carries the bare essentials.

DESIGNER

JULIE ROMINE

WHAT YOU NEED

- Basic Cozies Tool Kit (page 12)
- Scraps of coordinating cotton fabric
- Fusible lightweight interfacing
- Key ring
- Hook-and-loop tape
- One 3/4-inch (1.9 cm) button
- Carabiner

SEAM ALLOWANCE

1/4 inch (6 mm) unless otherwise noted

WHAT YOU DO

1 Enlarge the template on page 122. Cut two rectangles from different fabrics for the cozy body and one rectangle from the interfacing. Cut four tab pieces.

2 For the closure tab: With right sides together, stitch the tab on three sides. Trim the seam allowance to 1/8 inch (3 mm), clip the corners, and turn right side out. Fold in the raw ends 1/2 inch (1.3 cm) and press the tab. Set aside.

3 For the key ring tab: With right sides together, stitch the tab on two sides. Trim the seam allowance to 1/8 inch (3 mm) and turn right side out. Fold in half lengthwise, slip the key ring into the fold, and press. Set aside.

4 Pin the body rectangles right sides together. Lay the interfacing on top with the fusible side facing down. Lightly mark where the tab will be placed—when you stitch on all sides, leave an opening there (wider than the tab) for turning. Trim the interfacing close to the stitch line to reduce bulk, clip the corners, turn right side out, and press flat.

5 Tuck in the seam allowance at the opening and pin the ends of the key ring tab in the opening. Baste in place with a 1/8- inch (3 mm) seam allowance.

6 Fold the body piece in half with the fabric you want showing on the outside. Press to make a crease. Fold the short sides to create the card slots and press. Open up the body piece and lay it flat with the outside fabric facing up. Using the crease lines as a guide, place the closure tab and hook-and-loop tape according to the template and stitch them in place (figure 1). Use a boxstitch (as shown) to secure the tab.

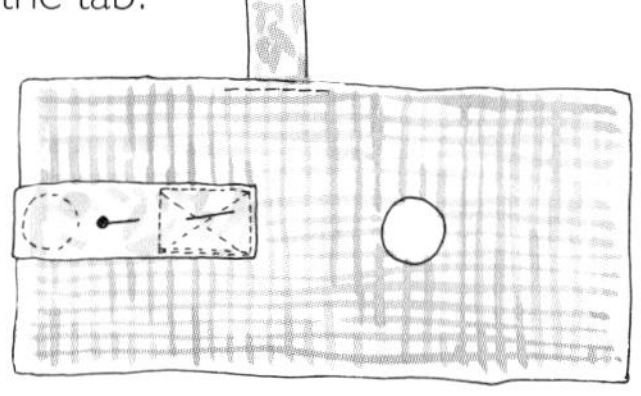

figure 1

7 Refold the side flaps and pin. Stitch them in place by running a 1/8 inch (3 mm) seam all the way down on both sides.

8 Sew hook-and-loop tape on the inside of the closure tab, checking that it aligns with the other half of the tape. Hand sew a button on the outside of the closure tab to hide the stitches for the hook-and-loop tape. Attach a carabiner to the key chain and you're all set to go shopping.

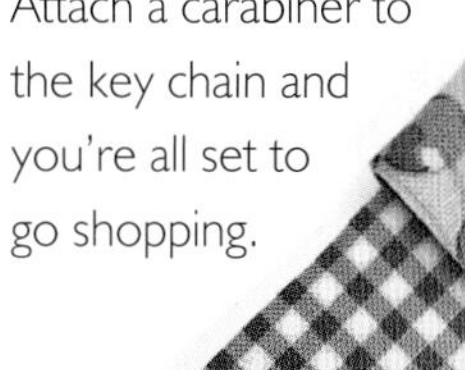

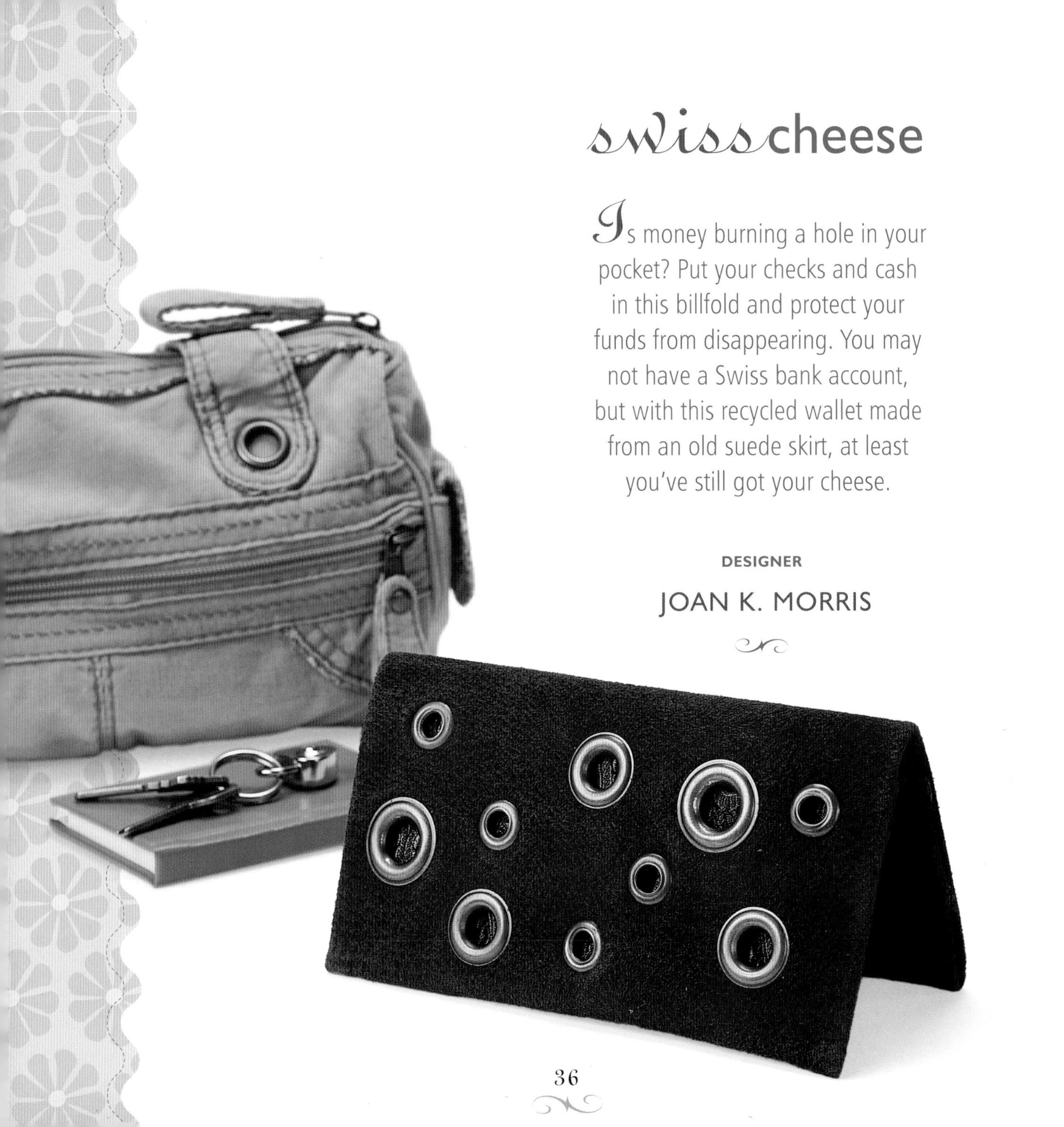

swiss cheese

Is money burning a hole in your pocket? Put your checks and cash in this billfold and protect your funds from disappearing. You may not have a Swiss bank account, but with this recycled wallet made from an old suede skirt, at least you've still got your cheese.

DESIGNER

JOAN K. MORRIS

WHAT YOU NEED

- Basic Cozies Tool Kit (page 12)
- 1 used suede skirt or jacket, or 7 x 14-inch (17.8 x 35.6 cm) piece of suede
- Strong glue suitable for leather
- 6½ x 7-inch (16.5 x 17.8 cm) piece of stiff stabilizer fabric
- Basting glue stick
- Assortment of antique brass grommets, different sizes
- Leather hole punch
- Grommet set
- 6½ x 7-inch (16.5 x 17.8 cm) piece of silk or other fabric for the liner
- Toothpick

WHAT YOU DO

1 If you're starting with an old jacket, cut a 7 x 14-inch (17.8 x 35.6 cm) piece of suede from it. Turn the short sides under ½ inch (1.3 cm). Stitch in place or use leather glue.

2 Fold the stabilizer fabric in half so the 6½-inch (16.5 cm) ends meet. Draw a line at the fold and crease the fold well. Find the center of the suede piece along the length. Mark the fold on both sides with a pen. Line up the center of the stabilizer with the center of the suede, leaving ¼ inch (6 mm) on each side (figure 1). Use the basting glue to keep the stabilizer in position.

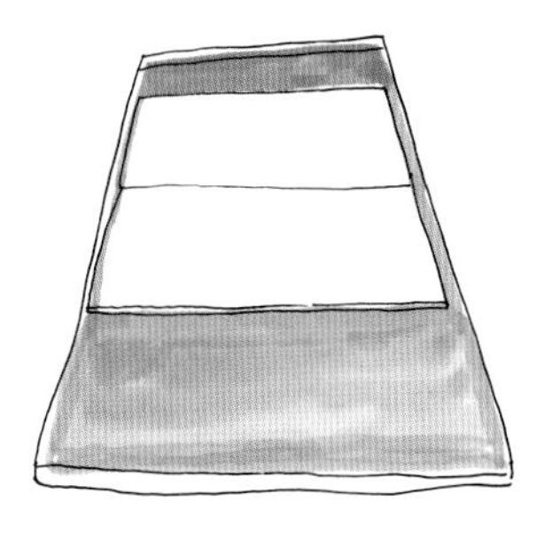

figure 1

3 Turn the suede right side up and lay out the grommets, keeping them within the area backed by the stabilizer. Trace inside each grommet to mark where it goes, remove the grommets, and use the hole punch to open up each circle. (Punch twice for the larger grommets.) Follow the manufacturer's instructions to install the grommets.

4 Place the silk fabric right side down on the wrong side of the suede, positioned over the stabilizing fabric. Use basting glue to hold the silk in place. Fold the ¼-inch (6 mm) sides over the top of the fabric and all the way down both sides. Apply leather glue with a toothpick to seal the fold.

5 To create the pockets that hold the checks and register, fold the outside edges of the suede to the inside. Use a small amount of glue to hold the edges down (too much glue may result in a lumpy, enlarged seam, making it difficult to insert checks). Fold the cozy in half at the center crease and weight it with a few books overnight or until the glue is dry.

undercover

Dear Diary, I haven't written in a while, but today I made you the prettiest case. Inside, I stitched a large pocket to slide you into. Opposite that are tabs for pen-holders and more pockets for note cards. Now, I have to tell you about this hottie I just met....

DESIGNER

HELEN ANGHARAD HENLEY

WHAT YOU NEED

Basic Cozies Tool Kit (page 12)

1/4 yard (22.9 cm) of linen

1/4 yard (22.9 cm) of cotton print

1/4 yard (22.9 cm) of cotton flannel or brushed cotton

1/2 yard (44.7 cm) of heavyweight fusible interfacing

6 inches (15.2 cm) of 1/4-inch (6 mm) gingham ribbon

1 button

SEAM ALLOWANCE

1/4 inch (6 mm) unless otherwise noted

WHAT YOU DO

1 Cut out the fabrics as follows.

- **From the linen**
  One 8 x 12-inch (20.3 x 30.5 cm) rectangle (outside of cozy)

  One 8-inch (20.3 cm) square (inside right pocket)

- **From the cotton print**
  One 8 x 12-inch (20.3 x 30.5 cm) rectangle (interior of cozy)

  One 8 x 11-inch (20.3 x 27.9 cm) rectangle (inside left diary flap)

  One 8 x 6-inch (20.3 x 15.2 cm) rectangle (inside right pocket)

  One 3 1/2 x 5-inch (8.9 x 12.7 cm) rectangle (penholder)

  One 3 1/2 x 8-inch (8.9 x 20.3 cm) rectangle outside embellishment panel)

- **From the cotton flannel**
  One 8 x 12-inch (20.3 x 30.5 cm) rectangle (padding)

- **From the interfacing**
  One 8 x 11-inch (20.3 x 2.9 cm) rectangle

  One 8-inch (20.3 cm) square

  One 8 x 6-inch (20.3 x 15.2 cm) rectangle

  One 3 1/2 x 5-inch (8.9 x 12.7 cm) rectangle

  One 3 1/2 x 8-inch (8.9 x 20.3 cm) rectangle

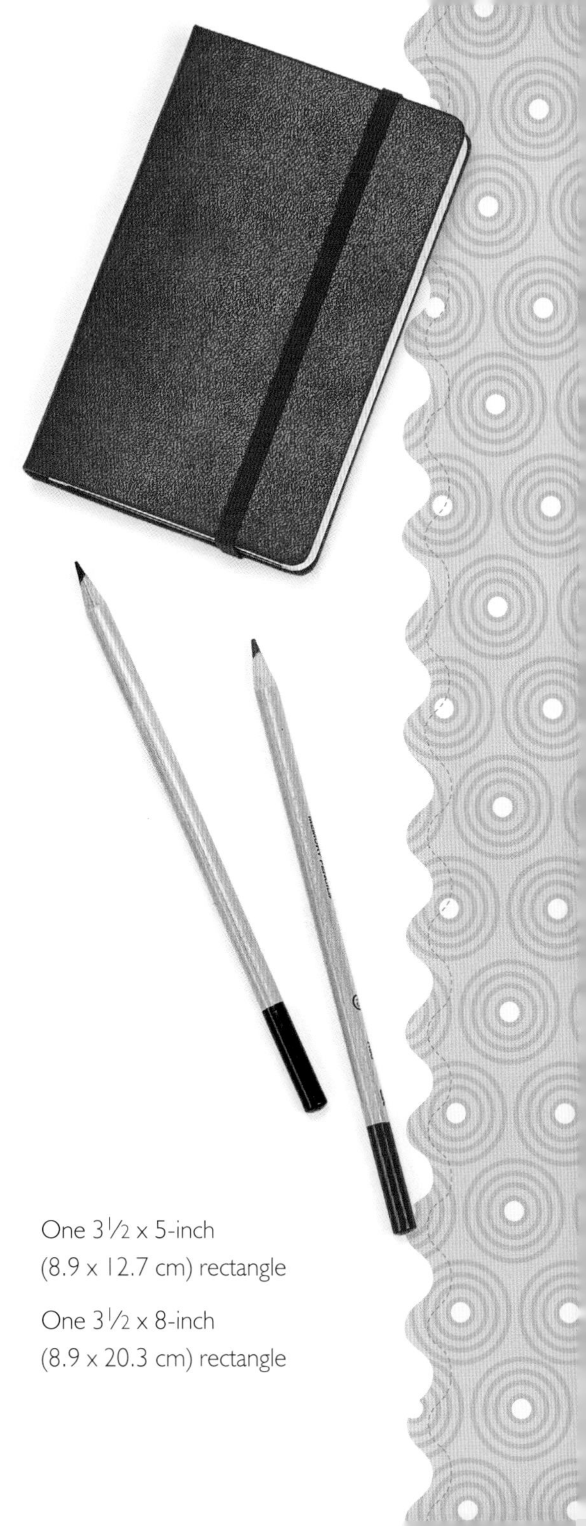

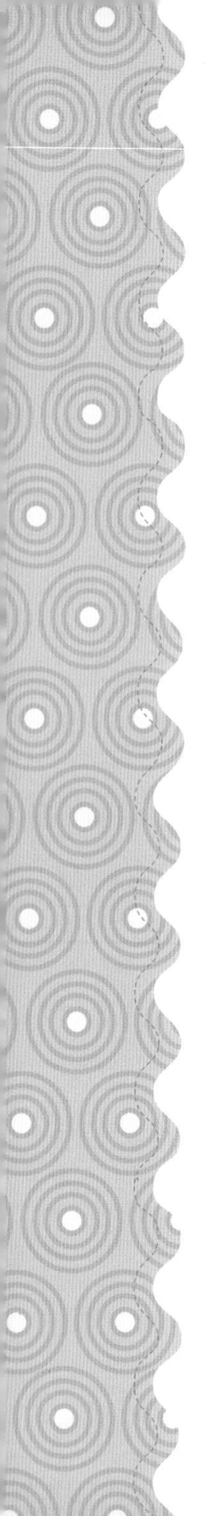

2 Following the manufacturer's instructions, fuse the interfacing to the wrong side of all pieces cut from the cotton print fabric, except for the interior of the cozy. Also fuse interfacing to the wrong side of the linen inside pocket square.

3 To make the inside right pocket panel, fold the cotton piece in half lengthwise, wrong sides together, to make an 8 x 3-inch (20.3 x 7.6 cm) piece. Press and then edgestitch along the folded edge. Do the same for the linen pocket square, folding it in half and edgestitching the fold. With both sides facing up, pin the cotton piece on top of the linen, aligning them on the right. Measure to find the midway point and stitch across the cotton fabric. Set aside.

4 To make the inside left diary flap, fold the piece in half as in step 3, making an 8 x 5½-inch (20.3 x 14 cm) folded piece. Press and stitch the folded edge as before. Set aside.

5 To make the penholder, press under the edges of the fabric ¼ inch (6 mm) on all sides. Fold it in half lengthwise, wrong sides together, and edgestitch on all four sides. Set aside.

6 To embellish the cozy exterior: with both sides facing up, lay the cotton flannel piece lengthwise left to right, and pin the linen rectangle on top. Press under ¼ inch (6 mm) on the two long sides of the embellishment panel. Measure 2 inches (5.1 cm) from the right edge of the linen rectangle and position the edge of the panel there, aligning the short edges with the edges of the linen. Pin in place and topstitch all four sides of the panel as close to the edge as possible, stitching through all layers. Stitch a series of parallel lines across the panel, using the edge of your presser foot as a guide.

7 Assemble the pieces by first laying out the interior cotton piece, right side up. For the penholder placement, mark with a pin or chalk where the cozy will fold in the middle. The left edge of the penholder will be positioned at the fold about 2 inches (5.1 cm) from the top edge of the cozy. Mark this spot.

Press under both short ends of the penholder ½ inch (1.3 cm). Pin one end at the fold where marked, and pin the other end 2¾ inches (7 cm) to the right, which leaves some slack in between. Stitch a narrow rectangle over the folds at both ends. Place two pens under the loop of fabric to mark where you need to stitch the slots. Stitch a small rectangle through all the layers at this central point (figure 1).

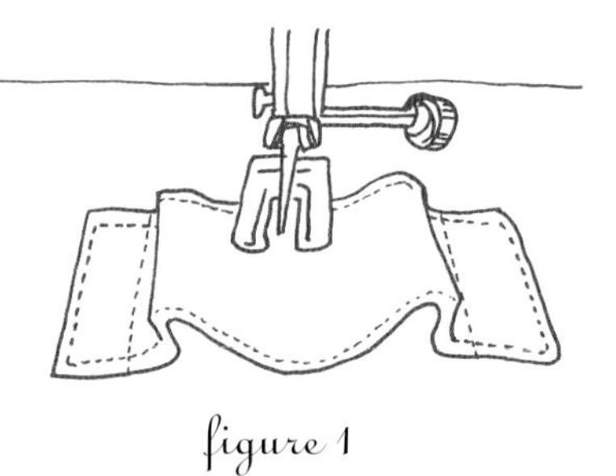

figure 1

8 Pin the left flap and the right pocket panel to the right side of the interior, aligning the outer raw edges. (The left edge of the pocket panel will slightly overlap the penholder strip.) Baste the pocket pieces in place.

9 Fold the gingham ribbon in half to form a loop. Pin the ends at the halfway point on the right-hand side pocket and baste in place. Pin down the folded end to keep it out of the way.

10 Lay the exterior cozy piece on top of the interior and pocket pieces with the right sides facing. Position the side with the embellishment to the left (figure 2).

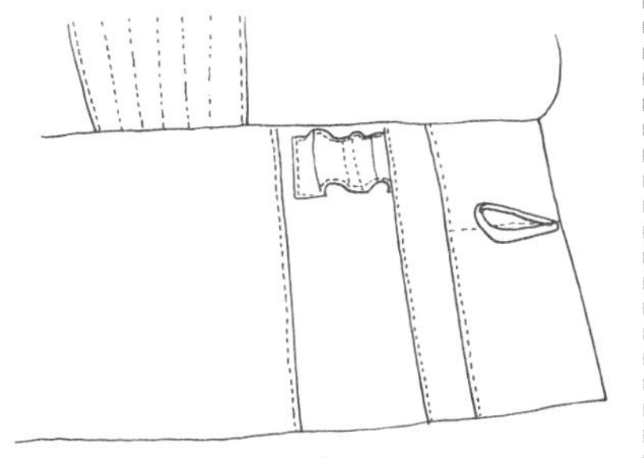

figure 2

Pin the layers together and start stitching on the left-hand side about 2 inches (5.1 cm) from the top edge of the fabric. Stitch through all layers all the way around the cozy, leaving a 3-inch (7.6 cm) opening for turning.

11 Clip the corners, trim the seam allowance, and turn the cozy right side out through the opening. Push out the corners and press the cozy inside and out, turning in the seam allowance at the opening. Edgestitch all the way around the cozy, closing the opening.

12 Fold the cozy closed and mark where the button needs to be aligned with the ribbon loop. Hand sew the button in place.

zippin' along

You're smack dab in the middle of crafting inspiration when it hits: Where are my scissors? Instead of accusing everyone in the household, simply zip it.

DESIGNER

JOAN K. MORRIS

WHAT YOU NEED

Basic Cozies Tool Kit (page 12)

1/4 yard (22.9 cm) of thick woven fabric

9 zippers, assorted colors, any lengths

18 inches (45.7 cm) of cording

SEAM ALLOWANCE

1/4 inch (6 mm) unless otherwise noted

WHAT YOU DO

1 Enlarge the template on page 123. Check the size against your scissors and make any necessary adjustments, remembering to include the seam allowance. Cut two pieces from the woven fabric.

2 On each of the zippers, zigzag the top closed above the zipper head. To avoid breaking your needle, don't use the foot pedal. Instead, "walk" the needle across the zippers by rolling the hand wheel on the right of the machine. Lay the zippers across one of the fabric pieces as shown in figure 1, alternating the heads of the zippers. Place each zipper head with the top 3/4 inches (1.9 cm) from one edge of the fabric and mark a line on the zipper just beyond where it overlaps the opposite edge. The bottom zipper has no head, and can be cut from the other zipper ends.

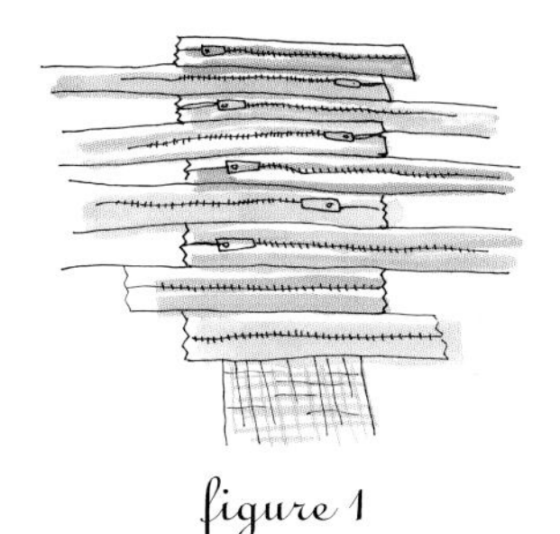

figure 1

3 Starting with the top two zippers, line up the marks you made and use a tight zigzag stitch to join them with the edges butted together. Your sewing foot should fit between the zipper heads, but if it doesn't, just unzip them and move the heads. Repeat with each zipper to the bottom.

4 Place the joined zippers on top of a woven fabric piece and stitch them together very close to the edge down both sides. Cut away the unnecessary zipper ends. With a tight zigzag, stitch the edges of the top and bottom zippers to the fabric.

5 With right sides together, pin the two fabric pieces and stitch 1/4 inch (6 mm) from the side edges, down one side, around the bottom point, and up the other side. Finish the side seams by running a zigzag stitch down the length of the seam allowance on the sides and trimming any excess fabric, especially at the narrow end of the cozy.

6 Turn the piece right side out, and push out the narrow end. Leave the bottom zipper inside—this adds protection to the bottom where the scissor point goes in. Hand sew the bottom shut along the edge of the bottom outside zipper. Zigzag the top back edge of the cozy to match the zigzag edge on the front.

7 Fold the cording in half and stitch the ends to the inside top of the copy, using a zigzag stitch.

diapersnug

DESIGNER

SARAH LALONE

Taking Baby places this afternoon? Those humble diapers deserve more than a ho-hum case. Packed in this tote, they'll never get stuffed at the bottom of your wee one's travel bag.

WHAT YOU NEED

Basic Cozies Tool Kit (page 12)

½ yard (45.7 cm) of quilting-weight cotton (interior)

½ yard (45.7 cm) of complementary quilting-weight cotton (exterior)

½ yard (45.7 cm) of lightweight fusible interfacing

One ¾-inch (1.9 cm) button

WHAT YOU DO

1 Cut two 8 x 18-inch (20.3 x 45.7 cm) rectangles from both fabrics and the fusible interfacing. From the exterior fabric, also cut one 3 x 10-inch (7.6 x 25.4 cm) strip for the strap. From the interior fabric, cut one 1¼ x 3-inch (3.2 x 7.6 cm) strip for the button loop.

2 To make the strap, press the fabric strip in half lengthwise to make a crease. Press under each long side into the center crease and press. Refold the center crease, press, and topstitch (page 20). Fold the strap in half, press, and set aside (figure 1).

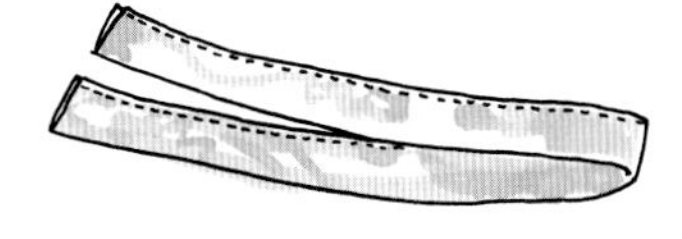

figure 1

3 Make the button loop in the same way as the strap in step 2. Fold into a loop as shown (figure 2), press, and set aside.

figure 2

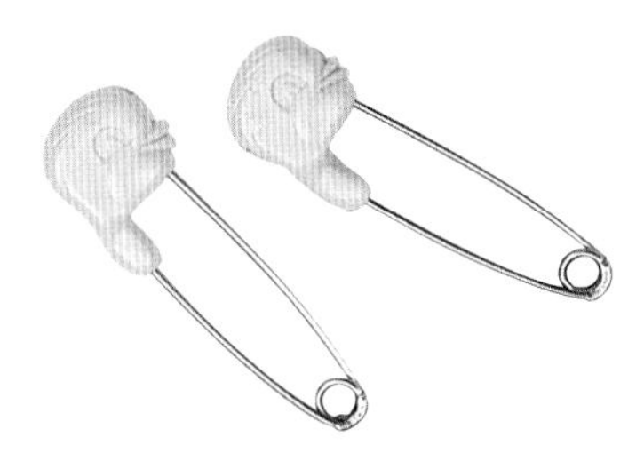

4 Following the manufacturer's instructions, fuse the interfacing to the wrong side of each exterior piece of fabric. With right sides facing, pin the exterior pieces together on two long sides and one short side—the unpinned side will become the top. Measure 9 inches (22.9 cm) from the top to find the halfway point on one long side of the bag. At that spot, slip the folded strap between the two pieces and pin the raw ends in line with the edge of the bag. Stitch the three pinned sides and through the strap. Press the seams open and set aside.

5 To make the lining: With right sides facing, pin the interior rectangles together on three sides, again leaving one short side open. Stitch and press the seams open.

(continued on next page)

6 With both the exterior and the lining wrong side out, make boxed corners as follows:

- Cut a 1-inch (2.5 cm) square out of the bottom corners (figure 3).

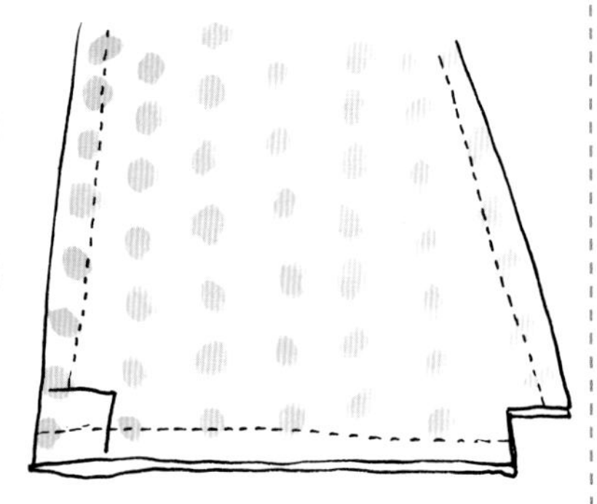

figure 3

- Refold the corners to bring the cut edges together, aligning the side and bottom seams in the middle. Pin and stitch (figure 4). Trim the seam allowance to 1/4 inch (6 mm).

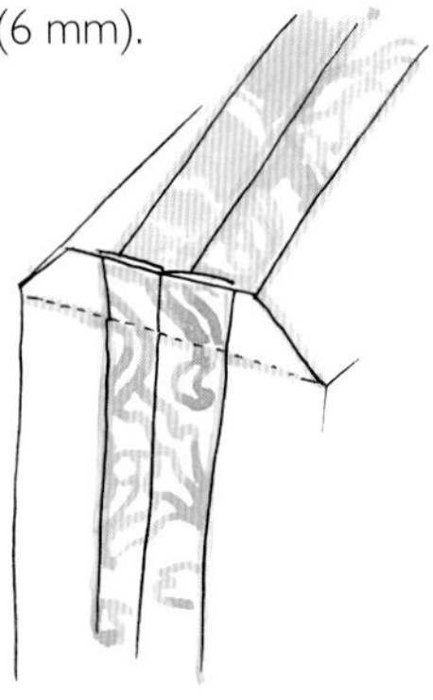

figure 4

7 For both the exterior and lining, press under the top edge 1 inch (2.5 cm). Turn the exterior right side out, and with the lining wrong side out, slip the lining into the exterior. Pin the top edges together.

8 Position the pouch with the wrist strap to the right, and locate the center of the back top edge. Tuck the raw ends of the loop between the exterior and the lining, with the loop extending outward. Edgestitch all the way around the top and through the loop.

9 Fold over the top 6 inches (15.2 cm) of the bag and press a crease for closing the pouch. On the front of the bag below the fold, mark the middle of the loop for the button placement, and hand sew the button in place.

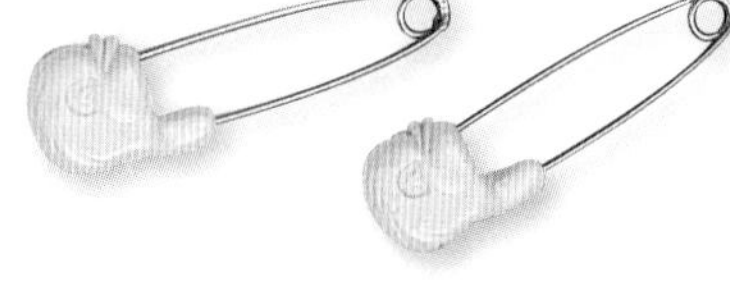

book nook

DESIGNER

MORGAN MOORE

What do bookworms, night owls, and children have in common? They all want this clever carrier! Slip your books and magazines into the canvas compartments when it's time to drift off to dreamland.

WHAT YOU NEED

Basic Cozies Tool Kit (page 12)

1½ yards (137.2 cm) of canvas

2½ x 15-inch (6.4 x 38.1 cm) piece of fabric to bind the larger pocket

1½ x 11-inch (3.8 x 27.9 cm) piece of fabric to bind the smaller pocket

Four 4½-inch (11.4 cm) squares of assorted fabrics for the letters

¼ yard (22.9 cm) of paper-backed fusible web

WHAT YOU DO

1 Cut the canvas.

Piece A: 52 x 15½ inches (132.1 x 39.4 cm)

Piece B: 14½ x 15½ inches (36.8 x 39.4 cm)

Piece C: 9½ x 10½ inches (24.1 x 26.7 cm)

2 Hem the long edges of canvas piece A by folding them under ¼ inch (6 mm), pressing, folding them over again ¼ inch (6 mm), and stitching.

3 To bind the top edge of the larger pocket, fold under both long sides of the larger pocket—binding fabric ¼ inch (6 mm). Insert a shorter side of canvas piece B into one the folded edges (figure 1).

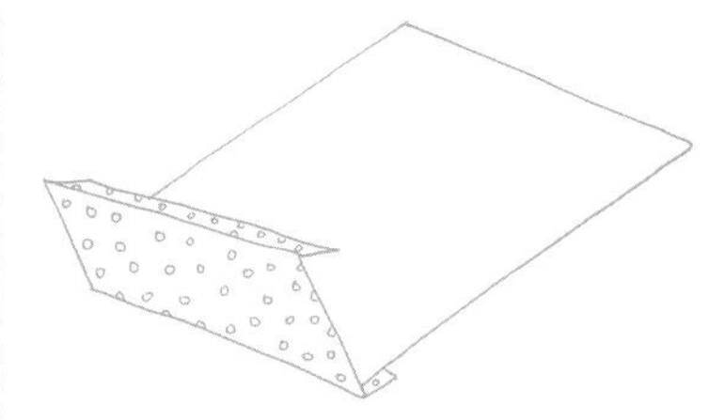

figure 1

Fold and pin the binding fabric so it conceals the edge of the canvas; then topstitch close to the edge and press. Stitch the opposite edge of the pocket trim to the canvas, stitching close to the trim's edge.

4 Using the C piece of canvas and the smaller piece of pocket trim, repeat step 3 to bind the edge of the smaller pocket.

5 Fold under the bottom of the smaller pocket—opposite the fabric binding—and the sides ¼ inch (6 mm) and use pins to hold the folds. Pin the pocket to the center of the larger pocket and topstitch close to all edges but the top.

6 Fold under the sides and bottom of the large pocket 1/4 inch (6 mm) and press. Pin the wrong side of the large pocket to one end of the right side of piece A, matching the edges (figure 2). Topstitch along the edge of the pocket to attach it to piece A. Set aside.

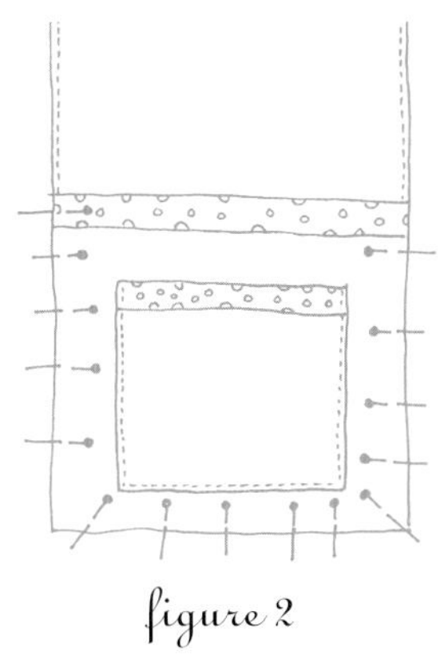

figure 2

7 Using a word-processing program, type the letters R, E, A, and D, and size the letters so they're 4 inches (10.2 cm) tall. Print them on heavy card stock and cut them out.

8 Follow the directions on the paper-backed fusible web to adhere it to the squares of fabric for the letters. Trace the card stock letters onto the fabric and cut them out. Remove the paper backing from the adhesive, position the letters on the canvas 3 inches (7.6 cm) from the top of the large pocket, and use a hot iron to attach them in place. Topstitch along the inner edge of the letters.

Place the finished cozy under your mattress. Sweet dreams!

BED MATES

To make a cozy that hangs from both sides of the bed, repeat these directions to make another identical element. Sew both elements together along the unadorned side.

spectacularcase

Seeing is believing. In this case, shades or specs look equally cool in soft velvet, and will help keep your lenses scratch-free. Branch out with some sleek little appliqués, and get your frame on.

DESIGNER

MARIA GORETTI YEN

WHAT YOU NEED

Basic Cozies Tool Kit (page 12)

Felt and fabric scraps

Optional: fray retardant (page 17)

8-inch (20.3 cm) square of velvet fabric

8-inch (20.3 cm) square of thin batting

8-inch (20.3 cm) square of liner fabric

SEAM ALLOWANCE

¼ inch (6 mm) unless otherwise noted

WHAT YOU DO

1 Cut an appliqué design to fit one side of the finished case, about 3 x 6½ inches (7.6 x 16.5 cm). To make the design shown, cut three ovals about 1 inch (2.5 cm) in diameter from the fabric scraps and cut branches from the felt. Don't worry about a pattern—freehand cutting will enhance the natural look. If you don't like the frayed look, use fray retardant on the pieces cut from fabric. (Felt doesn't fray.)

2 Fold the velvet square in half, wrong sides facing, to check how wide the case will be. Pin the design on one side, leaving at least ¾ inch (1.9 cm) of clearance on all sides for the seam allowance. Unfold the fabric and machine stitch along the edges of the appliqué pieces, removing pins as you sew. If you like, also do a freehand stitch inside the ovals to make sure they are secure.

3 Stitch the batting onto the back of the velvet as close to the outer edge as possible.

4 With right sides together, stitch the liner onto the batting-backed velvet. Start from the bottom, round off at the corners, and leave an opening at the bottom wide enough to turn the case right side out later (figure 1).

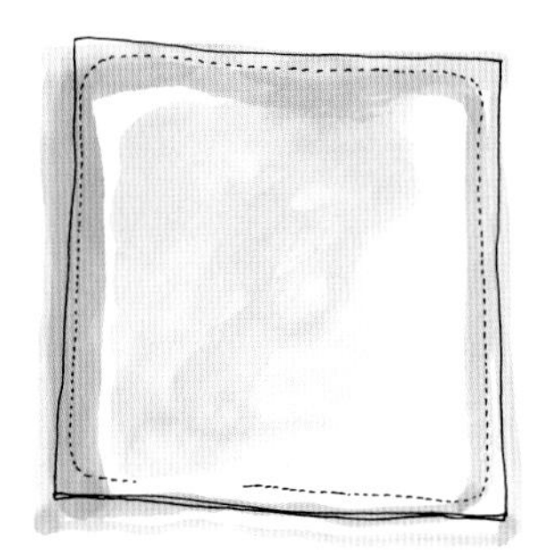

figure 1

5 Trim excess fabric off the corners and turn the case right side out. Hand sew the opening to close it.

6 Fold the case in half and pin it to form a sleeve with an opening at the top. Starting about 1 inch (2.5 cm) from the top, topstitch down the right-hand side, around the corner, and across the bottom (figure 2).

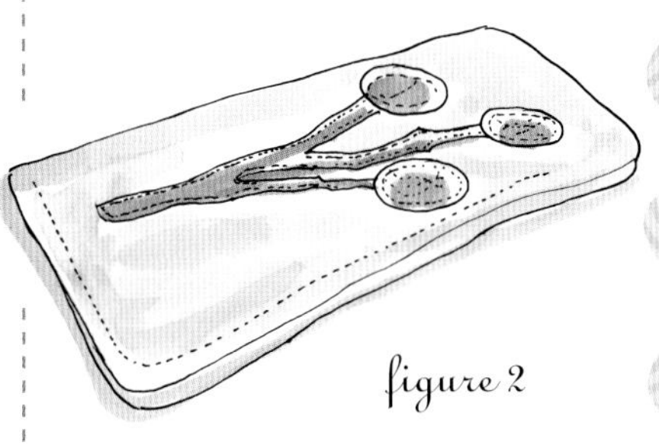

figure 2

spiffy SPF

DESIGNER

BETHANY MANN

When you worship the sun, do it safely. This little tote will carry all your sun block and lotion, and it even has a special spot for your lip balm. The interior of the bag is made from oilcloth so you never have to worry about spills.

WHAT YOU NEED

Basic Cozies Tool Kit (page 12)

1/4 yard (22.9 cm) of main fabric

2 coordinating fabric scraps

1/4 yard (22.9 cm) of oilcloth

1 yard (91.4 cm) of ribbon

SEAM ALLOWANCE

1/4 inch (6 mm) unless otherwise noted

WHAT YOU DO

1 Cut out the fabric as follows:

- From the main fabric, cut two rectangles that are 6 1/2 x 9 1/2 inches (16.5 x 24.1 cm). If the fabric is directional (like the one shown), make sure the pattern will be facing in the right direction (vertically).
- Cut a 2 1/4 x 3 1/2-inch (5.7 x 8.9 cm) piece from a fabric scrap, for the pocket.
- From another fabric scrap, cut a 6 1/2-inch (16.5 cm) square for the bottom.
- Cut one 6 x 22-inch (15.5 x 55.9 cm) rectangle from the oilcloth.

2 With right sides together, stitch the main fabric pieces on either side of the bottom piece (on the 6 1/2-inch [16.5 cm] sides) to make one long piece folded in half along its bottom.

3 To make the pocket, press under the bottom and two of the sides 1/4 inch (6 mm). Turn under the top edge 1/4 inch (6 mm) twice, press, and top-stitch. Pin the pocket wherever you like on the right side of the main fabric (leaving room for a seam allowance, if you place it to one side). Make sure the pocket is straight; then start stitching from the top of one side to the other.

(continued on next page)

4 Fold the oilcloth in half, shiny sides together. Stitch up both sides, and set aside.

5 Fold the exterior piece in half, right sides together. On each side, measure 2 inches (5.1 cm) from the top and mark the point with a pin or chalk. Stitch each side, leaving 2 inches (5.1 cm) open at the top. Press the seams open and turn the cozy inside out.

6 At each 2-inch (5.1 cm) opening, fold under the seam allowance twice as tightly as possible, stitch, and press (figure 1).

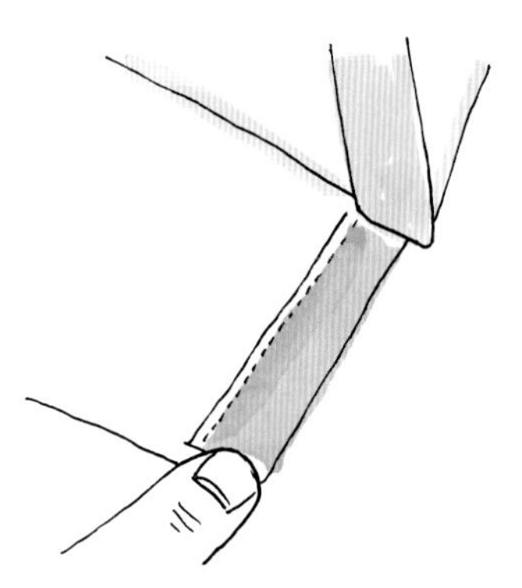

figure 1

7 To create the drawstring casing, press the top edge of the cozy under 1/4 inch (6 mm), and press under again 1 inch (2.5 cm). Turn the cozy right side out and slide the oilcloth liner inside the bag (wrong sides together). Pin and stitch the pressed edge over the top of the raw end of the oilcloth.

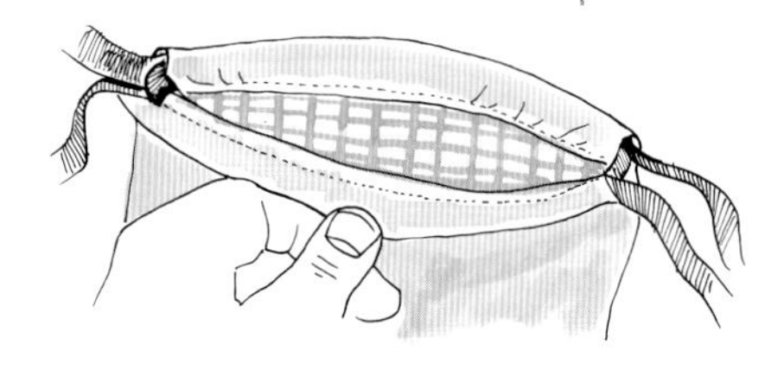

figure 2

8 Cut the ribbon into two 18-inch (45.7 cm) pieces. Attach a safety pin to the end of one piece and guide it through one side of the drawstring casing, past the opening on the other side and back again. Overlap the raw ends and stitch. Do the same with the other ribbon. Pull both ribbon seams into the casing so they don't show. To close the bag, pull one ribbon to the left and the other to the right (figure 2).

Pack your bags and head for the beach!

crafty carrier

This is the perfect accessory for crafters on the go. Pockets galore hold brushes, needles or hooks, scissors, and more. Roll it up, tie a knot, and hit the road.

DESIGNER

SARAH LALONE

WHAT YOU NEED

Basic Cozies Tool Kit (page 12)
1/2 yard (45.7 cm) of quilting-weight cotton (interior)
1/2 yard (45.7 cm) of complementary quilting-weight cotton (exterior)
1/2 yard (45.7 cm) of fusible fleece

WHAT YOU DO

1 Cut a 9 x 12-inch (22.9 x 30.5 cm) rectangle from both fabrics and the fusible fleece. From the exterior fabric, also cut two 1 1/2 x 12-inch (3.8 x 30.5 cm) strips for the ties. From the interior fabric, cut one 5 x 12-inch (12.7 x 30.5 cm) rectangle for the interior pocket panel.

2 To make each tie, fold over one short end 1/4 inch (6 mm) and press. Fold the strip in half lengthwise to make a crease. Fold each long edge into the center crease and press. Refold the center crease, press, and topstitch (page 20). Form a knot in the tie, close to the stitched end. Set aside.

3 Following the manufacturer's instructions, fuse the fleece rectangle to the wrong side of the exterior piece of fabric. Set aside.

4 To make the interior pocket panel, press under the top edge 1/4 inch (6 mm), press under another 1/2 inch (1.3 cm), and stitch. With both right sides facing up, position the pocket on the interior piece, aligning the bottom edges. Pin the pieces together on the sides. With a water-soluble fabric marker or chalk pencil, draw guidelines for sewing the slots (see box), and stitch. Baste very close to the outermost edges on both sides.

5 To put it all together, start with the interior piece, right side up. Pin the raw ends of both ties on the right side, just above the pocket as shown (figure 1). Lay the exterior piece on top, right side down, fleece facing up.

6 Stitch all the way around through all the layers, leaving a 3-inch (7.6 cm) opening along the top for turning.

7 Trim the corners (page 20) and seam allowances, and turn the project right side out. Turn under the raw edges at the opening and edgestitch or hand sew the opening closed.

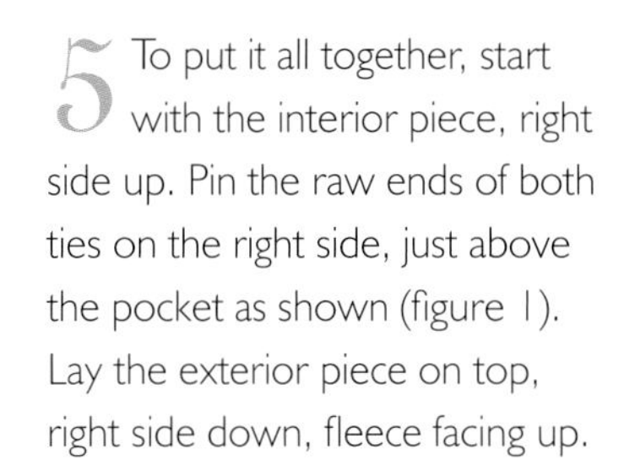

figure 1

POCKET SAVVY

When making the slots for the brush, you've got two choices:

1. Use these measurements, which will give you a variety of widths to fit your brushes: from the left side, measure 4 inches (10.2 cm), 5 inches (12.7 cm), 6 inches (15.2 cm), 7 inches (17.8 cm), 8 inches (20.3 cm), 9 ½ inches (24.1 cm), and 11 inches (27.9 cm).

2. Customize the slot widths to fit specific brushes. In this case, lay out your brushes, measure the widths of each one, and add ease to allow for the width of each brush.

techhead

Cocoon your cell phone, game controls, or laptop in a snazzy cover-up.

computer snooze

DESIGNER

SARAH LALONE

You may not get away with wearing your PJs to work, but that doesn't mean your laptop can't. When it's time to call it a day, your computer will sleep soundly and look great doing it.

WHAT YOU NEED

Basic Cozies Tool Kit (page 12)

½ yard (45.7 cm) of home-decorator-weight cotton fabric

½ yard (45.7 cm) of medium-weight denim for the lining

Two ¾-inch (1.9 cm) buttons

WHAT YOU DO

1 Measure the length, width, and height of your laptop. Cut two long rectangles, one from each fabric, based on this formula:

Length = (2 x length of laptop) + (2 x height of laptop) + 4 inches (10.2 cm)

Width = width of laptop + (2 x height of laptop) + 1½ inches (3.8 cm)

2 Pin the rectangles right sides together. At one of the short ends (which will become the flap), cut out a section on each side that is ¾ inch (1.9 cm) wide and 4 inches (10.2 cm) long from the top edge. Stitch around the edges, following the lines of the fabric and leaving a 4-inch (10.2 cm) opening on one side for turning. Trim all the outward corners and clip into the inward corners (figure 1).

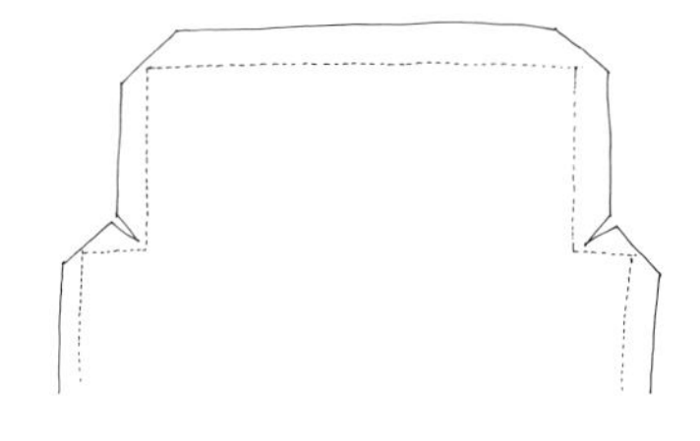

figure 1

3 Turn the project right side out through the opening and press flat. Fold under and pin the seam allowances at the opening. With right sides facing (denim facing out), fold the project in half lengthwise as far as the flap. Pin the sides and edgestitch (page 21) down both sides, backstitching at each end. Turn the cozy right side out.

4 On the front top/opening, measure 2 inches (5.1 cm) from the top and 2 inches (5.1 cm) from each side. Mark these points with a fabric marker and make buttonholes parallel to the top wide enough to fit your buttons (figure 2).

figure 2

5 Put your laptop inside the case. Fold over the flap and tuck it under the edge with the buttonholes. Mark the center of the buttonholes and sew the buttons on the flap.

disc-oh!

DESIGNER

JOAN K. MORRIS

Turn the beat around! At least that's what your disc player will be singing if you make this upbeat cozy. Now you can boogie with your player in hand. Dig it?

WHAT YOU NEED

Basic Cozies Tool Kit (page 12)

1/4 yard (22.9 cm) of corduroy fabric

4-inch (10.2 cm) square scraps of three cotton print fabrics

Fusible web scraps

One 7-inch (17.8 cm) zipper

18 inches (45.7 cm) of decorative cording

WHAT YOU DO

1 Enlarge the template on page 123. From the corduroy, cut out the following pieces:

- Two circles, using the template as a guide
- One 2 1/4 x 11-inch (5.7 x 27.9 cm) rectangle
- Two 1 1/2 x 9-inch (3.8 x 22.9 cm) rectangles

2 Run a zigzag stitch close to the edges of all the corduroy pieces.

3 To apply the appliqués, follow the manufacturer's instructions to attach fusible web to the back of the three cotton fabrics. Use the template pieces to draw the following on the paper backings:

- Six small petals from one fabric
- Six larger petals from another fabric
- One small circle from the third fabric

VANISHING ACT

If you like, use "invisible" thread—made from nylon monofilament—to stitch the appliqués in place. You need only to use it in the top of the machine, with regular thread in the bobbin. As a result, you will see less of the stitches and more of the fabric pattern.

4 Place one of the corduroy circles right side up. Remove the paper backing from the small circle and place it in the center of the corduroy circle. Remove the backing from the small petals and position them on the large petals. Lastly, remove the backing from the large petals and position them evenly around the corduroy circle. Iron all appliqués in place. Stitch around each petal and the center appliqué piece, using a zigzag stitch.

(continued on next page)

5 For each of the 1½ x 9-inch (3.8 x 22.9 cm) corduroy strips, press under one long edge ½ inch (1.3 cm). Using a zipper foot, stitch the folded edge of the strips on either side of the zipper (figure 1), centering the zipper within the strips and matching the strips on both sides of the zipper.

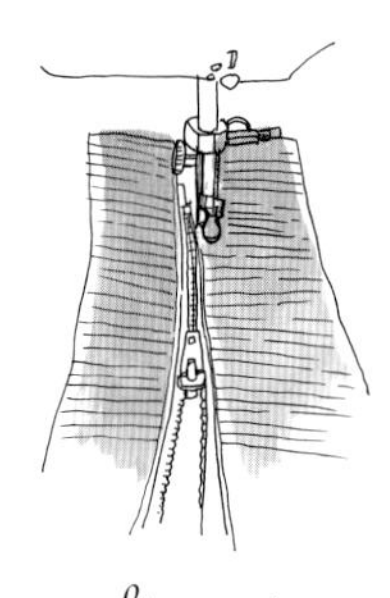

figure 1

6 At the top of the zipper, bring both strips together and pin them to the end of the 2¼ x 11 inch (5.7 x 27.9 cm) corduroy piece, right sides together. Leave a ½-inch (1.3 cm) gap above the zipper head. Stitch the pieces together and trim the strips to the same width, if necessary.

7 Fold the cording in half and pin the ends to the wrong side of the seam above the zipper head, with the looped cord aligned with the zipper. Stitch back and forth across the cording a few times to secure it.

8 With right sides facing, stitch the opposite ends of the two corduroy strips together to form a closed circle.

9 With right sides together, pin one edge of the zipper strip to the edge of the appliquéd corduroy circle. Stitch a ¼-inch (6 mm) seam around the perimeter, easing the zipper piece as needed.

10 Partially open the zipper. Pin the remaining corduroy circle in place and stitch as in step 9. Turn the cozy right side out through the open zipper, and bring the cording to the outside.

rapper wrapper

Doesn't matter whether you like hip-hop, metal, or jazz. Slip your media player inside this embroidered felt case and listen to your tunes in style.

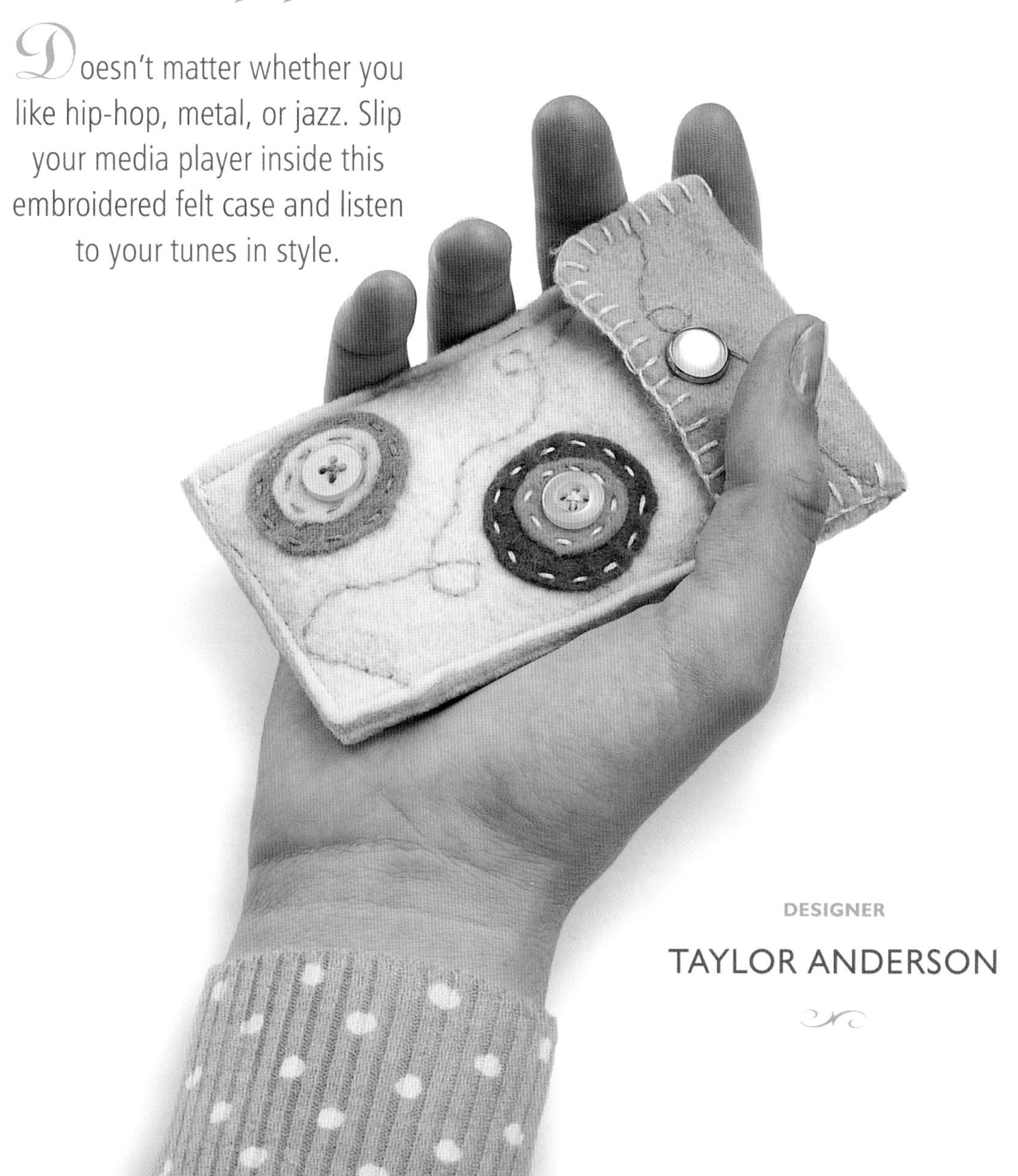

DESIGNER

TAYLOR ANDERSON

WHAT YOU NEED

- Basic Cozies Tool Kit (page 12)
- 9 x 12-inch (22.9 x 30.5 cm) piece of felt (main color)
- 9 x 12-inch (22.9 x 30.5 cm) piece of felt (second color)
- Felt scraps in a variety of colors
- 2 yards (182.9 m) of embroidery floss (main color)
- 1 yard (91.4 m) each of embroidery floss (other colors)
- 2 small 3/8-inch (9.5 mm) buttons
- 1 pearl-front snap
- Snap applicator and hammer

WHAT YOU DO

1 Cut rectangles measuring 3 x 4 inches (7.6 x 10.2 cm) and 3 x 6 inches (7.6 x 15.2 cm) from both large felt pieces. Pin the two larger pieces together and set them aside. Cut two 1 1/4-inch (3.2 cm) circles and three 1-inch (2.5 cm) circles from the felt scraps.

2 Plan the embellishment by laying out the felt circles on the 3 x 4-inch (7.6 x 10.2 cm) main color rectangle. The circles should be at least 1/4 inch (6 mm) away from the edges and low enough to allow for a 1 1/2-inch (3.8 cm) flap at the top. Use a running stitch (page 27) to attach the large circles to the felt. Sew the smaller circles on top, and sew the buttons on last. If you like, use embroidery floss to backstitch (page 27) a wavy, loopy line from the top left corner to the bottom right corner.

3 Pin the second 3 x 4-inch (7.6 x 10.2 cm) rectangle to the back of the embellished piece. Machine stitch the top only, as close to the edge as possible.

4 Attach the back of the snap to the center of the joined pieces, 1/4 inch (6 mm) away from the top stitched edge. Sew the remaining 1-inch (2.5 cm) felt circle to the back, behind the back of the snap (to prevent scratches).

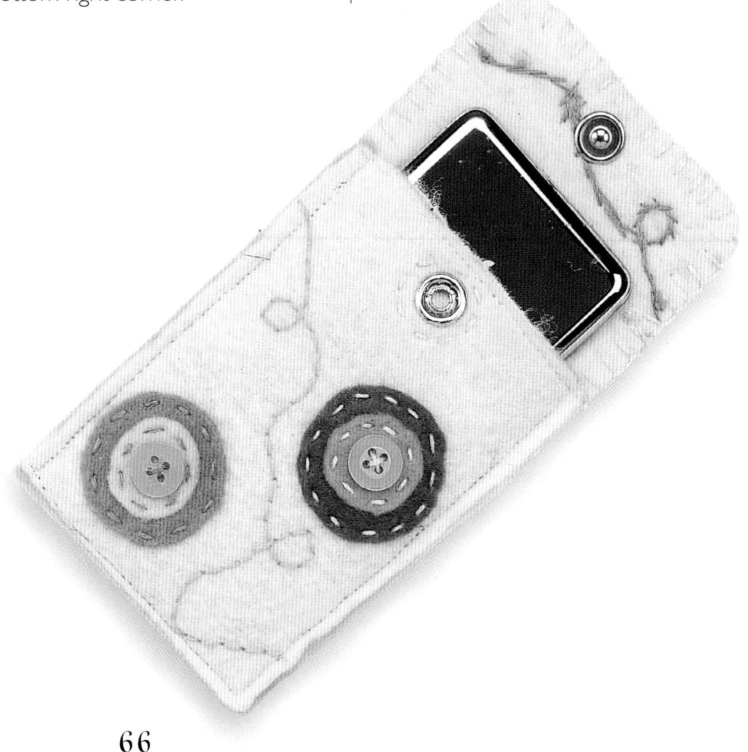

5 To identify what will be the flap, measure 1 1/2 inches (3.8 cm) from one end of the larger pinned rectangles. Within that space, on the color you want to be showing in front, backstitch another wavy, loopy line. Attach the front of the snap to that same side, 1/4 inch (6 mm) away from edge.

6 With wrong sides together, pin the front of the cozy to the back, with the flap of the larger piece extending past the top of the smaller piece. Stitch the sides and bottom as close to the edge as possible and trim any uneven areas.

7 Round off the corners of the flap; then blanket stitch around the edges of the flap. Insert your player and hit the road.

FREEWHEELING

If you want to access your media player while it's in the cozy, measure the size and position of the player's click wheel and screen. Cut corresponding holes through both layers of the paired rectangles. Reinforce the edges of these holes with a blanket stitch (page 27).

*line*up

Doesn't it drive you nuts, the way extra electronic cables get messy, tangled, or lost? In this case, it's so easy to keep them in line: Store the cords in stitched compartments that hold them neat, orderly, and under control.

DESIGNER

CHEYENNE GOH

WHAT YOU NEED

Basic Cozies Tool Kit (page 12)

2 x 22-inch (5.1 x 55.9 cm) piece of linen for the strap

13¾ x 19¾-inch (35 x 50.2 cm) piece of linen

14 x 19¾-inch (35.6 x 50.2 cm) piece of patterned fabric

FABRIC TIP

The size of this project is perfect for using fat quarters—those nifty sample cuts that are usually 18 x 21 inches (45.7 x 53.3 cm). You probably won't find linen cut to that size, but there are plenty of options for the patterned fabric.

WHAT YOU DO

1 To make the tie closure, fold the linen strip in half lengthwise to make a crease. Fold each long edge into the center crease and press. Refold the center crease, press, and topstitch (page 20). Stitch both ends of the tie and trim close to the seams to neaten them. Set aside.

figure 1

2 With right sides facing, pin the linen piece and the patterned fabric together. Stitch all four sides, leaving about 4 inches (10.2 cm) open on one of the shorter sides. Trim all four corners (page 20), and turn the cozy right side out through the opening. Fold under the raw edges at the opening to align with the rest of the seam, and edgestitch the entire side. Stitch the opposite side as well. These stitched edges are the top and bottom of the cozy. Choose one edge to be the top, and pin it as a reminder.

3 On the right (patterned fabric) side, measure 8 inches (20.3 cm) down from the top edge. Find the center of the cozy from the other direction, about 6½ inches (16.5 cm) from either side. Mark with a pin where these measurements intersect. Fold the tie closure in half and mark the center point. Unfold the tie and lay it on the patterned fabric with the ends going out to the sides (not top to bottom). Pin the center of the tie at the marked spot and stitch it to the cozy.

(continued on next page)

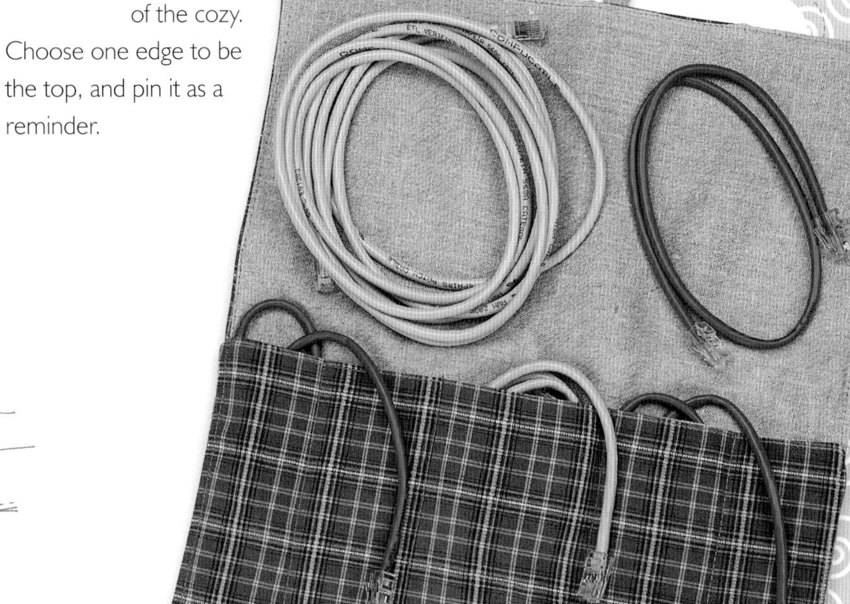

4 Turn the cozy over, with the linen side facing up. Fold the bottom edge up about 5½ inches (14 cm)—so it just covers the stitch line for the tie—and pin. Stitch both sides from the bottom corner to the top.

5 Before making the pockets, pull the ends of the tie closure over to the flap side and pin them down. This will keep them out of the way so you don't accidentally stitch them into the pocket seams. Measure about 2 inches (5.1 cm) from one side and mark with pins. From there, measure another 2½ inches (6.4 cm) and mark with pins.

Do the same from the other side. You will have marked four stitch lines for five pockets of varying widths (figure 2). Stitch each line from top to bottom. You now have a variety of pocket sizes for storing your cables.

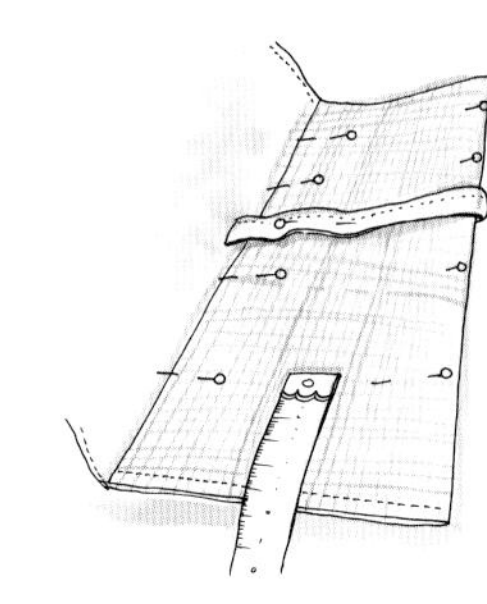

figure 2

*you*rang?

DESIGNER

BARBARA SHEPPARD

Cell-ebrate good times with a sassy carrier that keeps your phone at your fingertips. Made from vintage ties, it stitches up quick so you don't have to worry about going over your minutes!

WHAT YOU NEED

- Basic Cozies Tool Kit (page 12)
- Two 4-inch (10.2 cm) wide vintage neckties
- 10 x 14-inch (25.4 x 35.6 cm) piece of medium-weight fusible interfacing
- Bias strip maker (optional)
- Fabric glue
- 1 vintage-style button

SEAM ALLOWANCE

3⁄8 inch (9.5 mm) unless otherwise noted

WHAT YOU DO

1 Remove all stitching, interfacing, and lining from both neckties. Press. Decide which will be the outer fabric and which will be the lining.

2 Enlarge the templates on page 125. Cut both templates from the right side of the outer fabric and again from the wrong side of the lining fabric (figure 1). (The templates are cut this way so the strap pieces will match up correctly when placed wrong sides together.) Mark the location of the buttonhole.

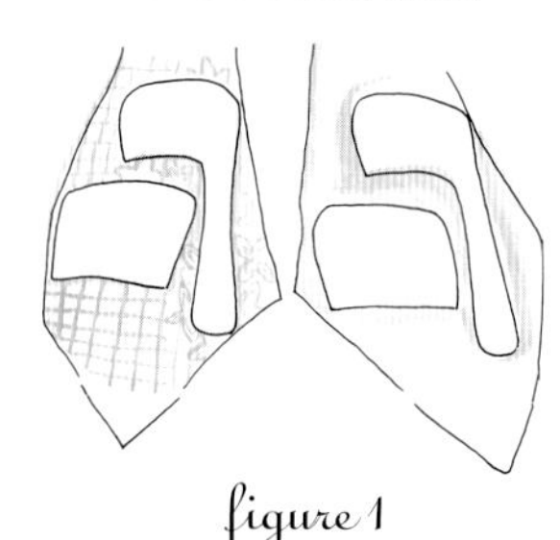

figure 1

3 Cut interfacing for the outer fabric only, making sure that the fusible side matches the wrong side of each piece. Follow the manufacturer's instructions for fusing.

4 Cut a 1 1⁄4 x 40-inch (3.2 x 101.6 cm) bias strip from the top part of the lining tie. (Since neckties are cut on the bias, it isn't necessary to cut strips on the diagonal.) Use a bias strip maker to make a 3⁄8-inch (1 cm) binding. If you don't own this handy gadget, press both raw edges to the center down the length of the bias strip, fold the strip in half lengthwise, and press again.

5 Stitch the front and back outer pieces together, ending the stitch line 1⁄4 inch (6 mm) from the raw edge on the side with the strap, as shown (figure 2). Make a small clip through the seam allowance to this stitching on the strap piece.

Trim the seams, press them open, and turn right side out. Do the same for the lining pieces, but don't turn them right side out.

figure 2

6 Place the lining inside the case with wrong sides together. Pin and baste around the raw edges. Make a buttonhole in the strap where marked.

7 Attach the binding to the raw edge with fabric glue. Plan for the raw ends of the binding to meet at the side seam without the strap, and turn them under. You'll need to stretch the binding a bit around the curved edge of the strap to keep it from puckering. (It's helpful to use clips to hold the binding until the glue dries.) Sew the button to the front of the case.

wild game

Don't be controlled by a style-less game remote—power up with fabulous holders. Give a little glam treatment, and you'll never again wonder where you put the controls.

DESIGNER

JOAN K. MORRIS

WHAT YOU NEED

Makes 2 control holders

Basic Cozies Tool Kit (page 12)

1/4 yard (22.9 cm) of tiger print faux fur

1/4 yard (22.9 cm) of leopard print faux fur

1/4 yard (22.9 cm) of heavyweight fusible interfacing

1/4 yard (22.9 cm) of satin for lining

1 yard (91.4 cm) of 1-inch (2.5 cm) beaded ribbon

ONE AT A TIME

These instructions are for making one game controller cover. To make the second, follow the same instructions, but switch the leopard and the tiger prints when cutting out the fabrics.

WHAT YOU DO

1 On the back of the tiger print, draw two 2 1/4 x 8-inch (5.7 x 20.3 cm) rectangles and cut them out. Also draw and cut out one 2 3/4 x 3-inch (7 x 7.6 cm) rectangle. On the back of the leopard print, draw one 2 1/4 x 8-inch (5.7 x 20.3 cm) rectangle and cut it out.

2 Lay the long pieces side-by-side, with the leopard print between the two tiger pieces. Make sure that the nap of the fur runs in the same direction. With right sides facing up, stitch two of the pieces together with a zigzag stitch (figure 1). Do the same with the third piece.

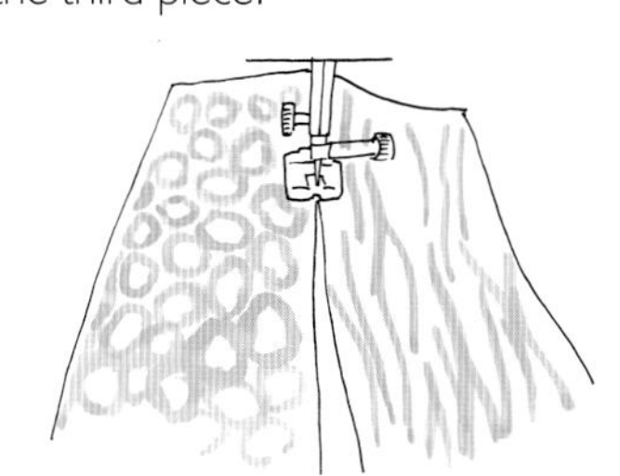

figure 1

3 Cut two 1 3/4 x 6-inch (4.4 x 15.2 cm) rectangles and two 1 1/2 x 6-inch (3.8 x 15.2 cm) rectangles from the interfacing. Position them on the back of the stitched fur piece alternating the rectangles: narrow, wide, narrow, wide. (figure 2):

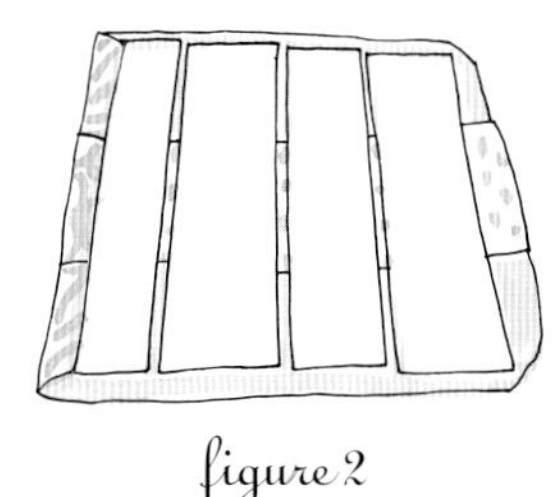

figure 2

- Line them up perpendicular to the seams.
- Center them on the fabric, leaving 1/2 inch (1.3 cm) on all sides for a seam allowance.
- Leave 1/4 inch (6 mm) between the rectangles.

Following the manufacturer's instructions, press the rectangles in place. Clip all four corners of the fabric at an angle and press under all four seams.

(continued on next page)

4 Cut a 7 x 8-inch (17.8 x 20.3 cm) piece of satin lining. Press under the edges ½ inch (1.3 cm) and lay it on the wrong side of the fur piece, covering the interfacing. Stitch in the three channels between the interfacing (figure 3). Hand sew around the entire outer edge to secure the satin lining to the fur exterior.

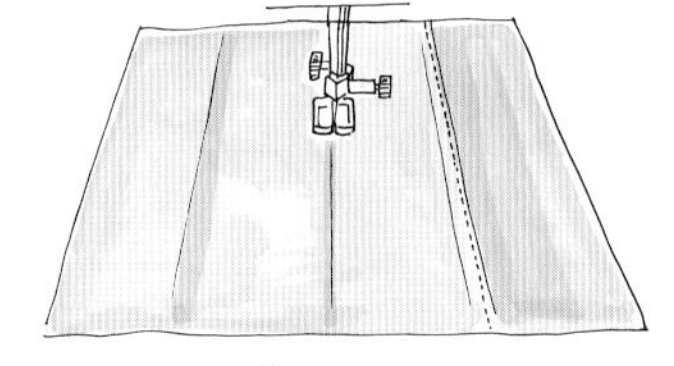

figure 3

5 Cut two 8-inch (20.3 cm) pieces of beaded ribbon. Center the ribbon along the seam line between the fur strips. Hand sew the edges of the ribbon in place. Bring the long sides of the fur piece together to form the box shape and hand sew the sides together.

6 Cut a 1¾ x 1½-inch (4.4 x 3.8 cm) piece of the interfacing. Center and press it to the wrong side of the remaining fur piece. Press under the seam allowances and hand sew in place at one end of the control holder.

picture perfect

When it comes to photographs, you want to look your best, but why leave your camera out of the picture? Protect it with a padded bag made from cushy corduroy and flannel. It's time you gave your camera a break—and we don't mean by dropping it.

DESIGNER

JOAN K. MORRIS

WHAT YOU NEED

- Basic Cozies Tool Kit (page 12)
- 6 x 12-inch (15.2 x 30.5 cm) piece of flannel
- 1/4 yard (22.9 cm) of corduroy
- 1/4 yard (22.9 cm) of medium weight sew-in interfacing
- 30 inches (76.2 cm) of 1/2-inch (1.3 cm) velvet ribbon
- 1 package of brown piping
- One 1/2-inch (1.3 cm) pearl-front snap
- Snap applicator and hammer

SIZE CONSIDERATIONS

This cozy is designed for a camera that measures 4 x 2 1/2 x 1 1/2 inches (10.2 x 6.4 x 3.8 cm). Alter the measurements as needed to fit your camera.

SEAM ALLOWANCE

1/4 inch (6 mm) unless otherwise noted

WHAT YOU DO

1 Cut out all of the pieces as follows:

- Enlarge the template on page 125. Cut two top pieces from the flannel.
- Cut four 3 1/2 x 5 1/4-inch (8.9 x 13.3 cm) front/back rectangles and two 2 1/2 x 12-inch (6.4 x 30.5 cm) side rectangles from the corduroy.
- Cut one top piece, two front/back rectangles, and one side rectangle from the interfacing.

2 To make the top, pin the flannel pieces right sides together and pin the top interfacing piece on a wrong side. Stitch up one side, pivot at the point, and stitch down the other side, leaving the bottom edge open. Clip the curves, turn right side out, and press flat.

Pin the ribbon on one side of the flap and stitch, easing the ribbon as you go (figure 1). Set the flap aside.

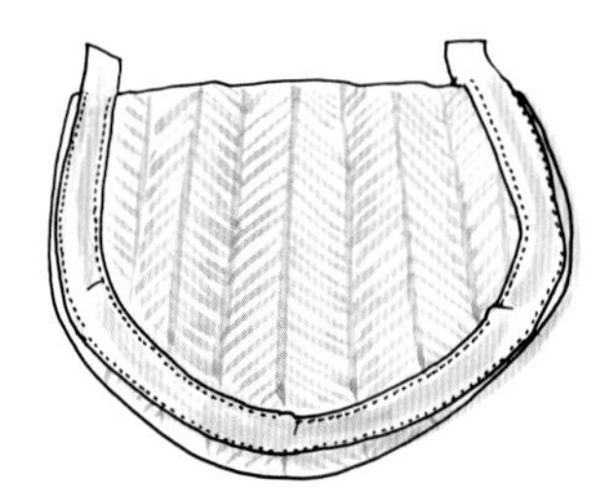

figure 1

3 For the outside of the camera case, pin each interfacing piece (front, back, and side) to the wrong side of a matching corduroy piece and baste all edges. (Set aside the remaining front, back, and side corduroy pieces for the lining.) On the right sides, pin the piping to both front/back pieces along three edges as shown (figure 2). Using a zipper foot, baste the piping in place.

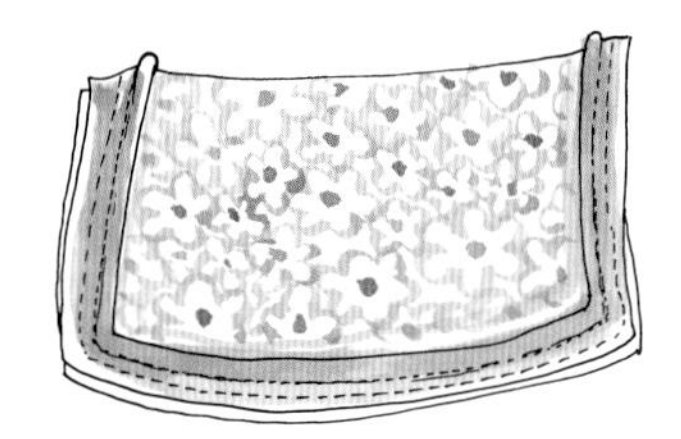

figure 2

4 With right sides together, pin the long side piece to a front piece along the piped edges. Using a zipper foot, stitch the pieces together, easing as you go. At each corner, leave the needle down, turn the piece, line up the edges, and continue stitching. Stitch the remaining front/back piece in the same way. Trim the seam allowances and turn the cozy right side out. Decide which side will be the front.

5 With right sides together, pin the bottom edge of the flap to the top of the back piece and baste. In the middle of each side of the case make a ¼-inch (6 mm) fold and baste. Cut a 16-inch (40.6 cm) piece of ribbon and fold it in half lengthwise with the right side facing out. On one of the sides, pin the ends of the ribbon on top of the fold and baste (figure 3).

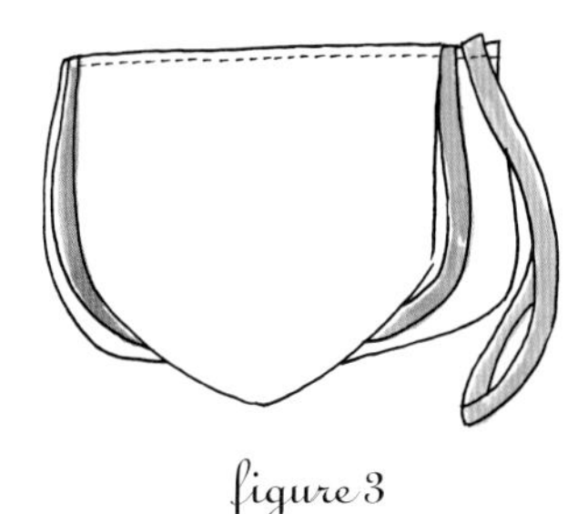

figure 3

6 To make the lining, stitch the three remaining corduroy pieces together in the same way as the outside of the camera cozy, but leave a 3-inch (7.6 cm) opening on one bottom edge.

7 With the case right side out and with right sides together, pin the lining over the case, leaving the flap and the ribbon in position between the case and the lining. On the sides, where the folds are, fold the lining to match. Stitch all the way around the top edge, stitching the flap and the ends of the ribbon in place as you go.

8 Pull the case through the hole in the lining, turning the whole thing right side out. Stitch the hole closed, stuff the lining into the cozy, and press the edges. Topstitch the sides only, moving the ribbon out of the way.

9 Following the manufacturer's instructions, attach the pearl side of the snap on the flap. Put your camera in the cozy, mark where the other side of the snap needs to be, and attach.

onhold

DESIGNER

MEREDITH GALLOWAY KISTNER

Snug your cell in a fleece case embellished with a stitched blossom and a leaf, and we bet you'll never leave it behind.

WHAT YOU NEED

Basic Cozies Tool Kit (page 12)

Fleece scraps in different colors

4 x 9-inch (10.2 x 22.9 cm) piece of fleece

WHAT YOU DO

1 Cut two circles for a flower and a leaf shape from the scrap fleece. The circles can be about 1 1/4 inches (3.2 cm) across and 1 3/4 inches (4.4 cm) across.

2 Fold the fleece in half lengthwise, to the shape that will fit the cell phone. Decide how you want to place the flower and leaf, allowing space around the design for a seam allowance. Unfold the fleece and stitch the pieces in place. Trim all excess thread.

3 Fold the fleece in half lengthwise again, but this time with the design on the inside. Stitch up both sides. Trim the seam allowances as close to the seam as possible and turn the cozy right side out.

sew clean

A sewing machine is the stitcher's greatest ally, so you want to keep it clean and in good working order. Keep dirt and fuzz at bay with a snazzy patchworked cover.

DESIGNER

BETHANY MANN

WHAT YOU NEED

- Basic Cozies Tool Kit (page 12)
- 1/2 yard (45.7 cm) of heavyweight cotton fabric
- Several strips of heavyweight cotton print fabrics
- 3/4 to 1 yard (68.6 to 91.4 cm) of lining fabric
- 3/4 to 1 yard (68.6 to 91.4 cm) of fusible interfacing

WHAT YOU DO

1 Measure the length, width, and height of your machine. (Use the widest part of each dimension.) Using figure 1 as a guide, you will make two rectangles (front and back) and one long side piece for both the exterior and the lining of the cozy. The additional inches (cm) are for 1-inch (2.5 cm) hems and 1/2-inch (1.3 cm) seam allowances.

2 Using the lining fabric, cut the side piece according to your measurements and cut two rectangles for the front and back. Cut matching pieces from the fusible interfacing. Following the manufacturer's instructions, fuse the interfacing to the wrong side of the lining. Set aside.

3 Cut the side piece from the heavyweight cotton fabric according to your measurements. To make the front and back, cut eight strips of heavyweight cotton fabric that are the correct height, with widths that add up to the total width. Don't forget to add a 1/2-inch (1.3 cm) seam allowance for each strip seam. It's better to cut strips that are a bit too wide, stitch them together (right sides facing), and then trim the rectangle to fit as needed. For variety, piece at least one of the strips with different colored rectangles. Press all seams open.

4 With right sides together, pin the side piece to the front panel. Snip a 3/8-inch (9.5 mm) notch at the top corners of the front piece to help ease the side strip around them. Stitch in place. Do the same with the back panel to make a fabric "box." Turn right side out and gently push out the corners. Stitch the lining pieces together in the same way.

5 For both the outer cozy and the lining, press under (to the wrong side) a 1-inch (2.5 cm) hem along the bottom. Slide the lining (wrong side out) into the outer cozy (right side out) so that wrong sides are together. Match up and pin the sides and corners. Stitch around the bottom edge to join the two together. Trim any hanging threads. Slide the cozy over your sewing machine and put your "baby" to bed.

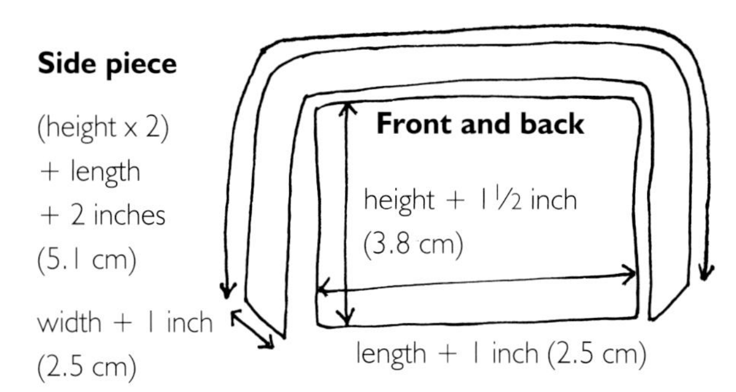

figure 1

scanner manner

DESIGNER

WENDI GRATZ

Camouflage an unsightly piece of equipment with a playful cover-up. Next time you scan a document, it will be a walk in the garden.

WHAT YOU NEED

Basic Cozies Tool Kit (page 12)

½ yard (45.7 cm) of cotton twill (main color)

¼ yard (22.9 cm) of cotton twill (second color)

Fabric scraps for the flowers

Scraps of paper-backed fusible web

1 package of jumbo rickrack

3 buttons

SEAM ALLOWANCE

¼ inch (6 mm) unless otherwise noted

WHAT YOU DO

1 Measure your scanner. Follow the Scanner Planner guide to work out the cozy dimensions and cut the two twill fabrics.

2 Enlarge the template on page 120. Trace the flower shapes onto the paper side of the fusible web. Cut them out, but not right on the lines—leave a little extra room all around the shapes. Following the manufacturer's instructions, adhere the web to the back of the fabric scraps. Cut out the flower shapes right on the lines and remove the paper.

Scanner Planner

For a custom fit, the scanner cozy measurements are based on the length and width of your scanner, plus the height, plus seam allowances. The main fabric will be three-quarters of the cozy and the second color one-quarter. Keep in mind that the cozy needs to be open across the back where the cords come out. Here's how to do the math:

Main fabric

- *Cut width = width of the scanner + (height of the scanner x 2) + 2 inches (5.1 cm) for side hems*
- *Cut length = length of the scanner x .75 (for three-quarters of the top) + 1¼ inches (3.2 cm) for top hem and seam allowance*

Second color

- *Cut width = same as the main fabric*
- *Cut length = length of scanner x .25 (for one-quarter of the top) + height of scanner + 1¼ inch (3.2 cm) for bottom hem and seam allowance*

3 Lay out the twill pieces, but don't sew them together yet. Arrange the flower appliqués and the rickrack on the main color. It's helpful to block off an area on each side equal to the height of the scanner + the 1-inch (2.5 cm) hem allowance. Lay a ruler or strip of paper at this mark (figure 1). This will help you place the appliqués on the top of the scanner and avoid having them fold over the sides.

figure 1

4 Pin the rickrack in place and then stitch it down. A single row of stitches down the middle of each strip will do.

5 With right sides together, stitch the main fabric to the second color, catching the raw edges of the rickrack in the seam.

6 Following the manufacturer's instructions, fuse the flower appliqués over the top ends of the rickrack stems. Stitch around the raw edges of the flowers, using a regular straight stitch. Hand sew a button in the center of each flower.

7 Hem all four sides of the scanner cozy by pressing under 1/2 inch (1.3 cm), then another 1/2 inch (1.3 cm). Stitch close to the folded edge.

8 Place the cozy face down over the scanner, with the hemmed edge hanging over the sides and bottom. (Remember that the back edge should not hang down.) Pin together the front corners of the cozy to form a box shape. Stitch across the corners as shown in figure 2, trim the seam allowance, then turn and press.

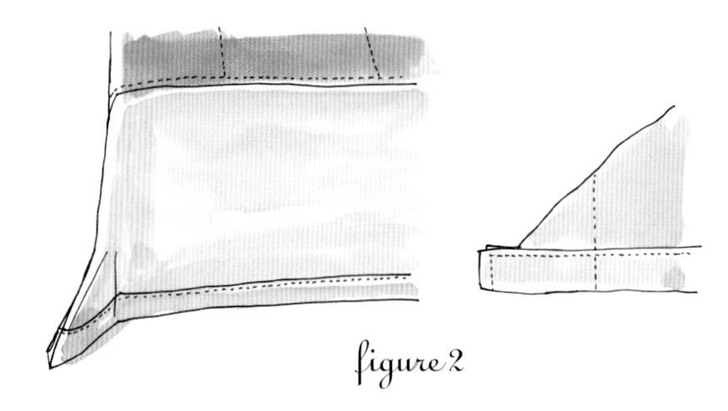

figure 2

off the cuff

To build a case suitable for a media player, start by snipping the sleeve off an old suit coat. Add a grommet for your ear bud cord. This little pouch will keep your player safe from scratches and accidental tumbles.

DESIGNER

CHEYENNE GOH

WHAT YOU NEED

- Basic Cozies Tool Kit (page 12)
- 1 used jacket or suit (the cuff should have buttons)
- 6¼ inches (15.9 cm) of black elastic thread
- ¼-inch (6 mm) grommet to match the jacket or suit
- Grommet set

WHAT YOU DO

1 Cut the jacket or suit sleeve 6 inches (15.2 cm) from the cuff edge. Cut or pick apart the seam opposite the cuff. Lay the fabric flat, right side facing up, keeping the lining in place. The buttons and cuff should be roughly in the middle.

2 Measure the length of your media player and add 1 inch (2.5 cm) for a seam allowance. This will be the length of the cozy. To make the buttons the center front of your cozy, measure the length of the cozy from the center of the button outward, on both sides (figure 1). Mark these edges with pins.

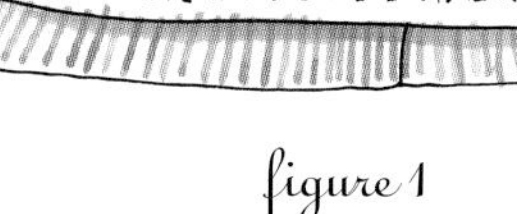

figure 1

3 Cut along the pinned lines and put the excess fabric to the side (to be used later).

Turn the cut sleeve so that the lining faces you. Gently pull the lining away from the fabric, but do not rip out the stitching that secures the lining to the cuff. No need to pull the lining away entirely, just enough to pin lining to lining and fabric to fabric, so you can make a seam opposite the button seam (figure 2). Stitch, and then fold the lining back to its original position.

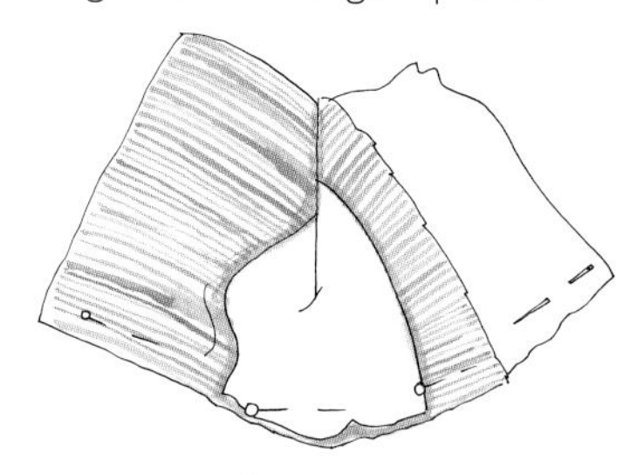

figure 2

4 Flatten the cuff with the button seam in the middle front, the opposite seam in the middle back, and folded edges on each side. Measure the width of your media player and add 1 inch (2.5 cm) for a seam allowance. Measure this distance from the finished edge of the cuff and mark with pins. Now make a French seam as follows:

- Stitch on the pinned line.
- Cut away the excess fabric very close to the stitch line.
- Turn the cozy inside out so that the inner lining is now exposed. Make sure the corners and seams are pushed out completely. Stitch close to the previous seam, enclosing it.

5 Turn the cozy right side out. On the back seam (opposite the button seam) decide where to attach the elastic thread. Hold down one end, and loop it around the first button and back again. Cut to this length, pin down the ends, and hand sew them onto the fabric (figure 3). This loop will have to bear a lot of strain, so make sure that your needle pokes through the elastic thread itself and not just around it.

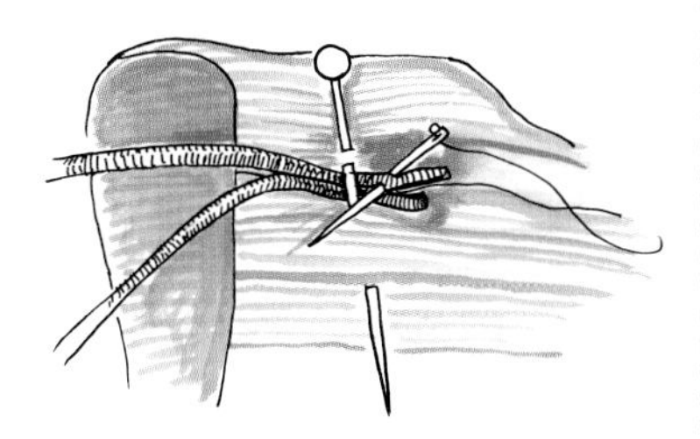

figure 3

6 With the excess fabric from step 3, cut a 1½ x 2¼-inch (3.8 x 5.7 cm) rectangle. Turn under all four edges for a neat patch to cover where the elastic is attached. Pin the patch in place and hand sew.

7 To make an outlet for the media player's earphone, make a mark ½ inch (1.3 cm) from the top edge of the cozy opening. Use a seam ripper to make a small opening; then use a pair of scissors to cut a small hole, no more than ¼ inch (6 mm) through both layers of fabric. Push the grommet with the longer crown through the hole from outside inward, and then hammer the grommet pair into place. This will ensure that the neat side faces outward.

kitchen stitchin'

When it comes to food and drink, these tasteful cozies help you keep your cool or handle the heat.

sweetstash

For a double shot of crafty cool, make your own cup hugger with a special stash pocket for your frequent sipper card, a teabag, or sugar packets. Break time has never been so sweet!

DESIGNER

GIGI THORSEN

WHAT YOU NEED

- Basic Cozies Tool Kit (page 12)
- 4½ x 12-inch (11.4 x 30.5 cm) scrap of outer fabric
- 4½ x 12-inch (11.4 x 30.5 cm) scrap of fleece 3-inch (7.6 cm) square of contrasting fabric for the pocket
- Fabric glue (optional)
- 1 decorative button

SEAM ALLOWANCE

¼ inch (6 mm) unless otherwise noted

WHAT YOU DO

1 Enlarge the template on page 121. Cut one piece from the outer fabric and one from the fleece.

2 With right sides together, pin the outer fabric to the fleece. Stitch the top and bottom edges. Trim the seam allowance, turn the cozy right side out, and press. Topstitch the top and bottom seams as close to the edge as possible.

3 Turn under all four sides of the pocket square ¼ inch (6 mm), using a few dabs of fabric glue if desired. Trim the folded corners with scissors so the excess doesn't peek out.

4 Mark the spot for the button placement, and sew the button to the pocket. Pin the pocket in place and stitch.

5 Place the ends of the cozy together, fleece side facing out. Use fabric glue or pins to hold in place, and stitch the ends together. Trim the seam allowance and finish the raw edges with a zigzag stitch. Time for a well-deserved coffee break.

good taste

After all the care you put into making that yummy casserole, you don't want it getting cold before serving. Bundled in a custom-fit wrap made from a sweet retro print, your dish will make it to the table steaming hot.

DESIGNER

ROBIN BEAVER

WHAT YOU NEED

Basic Cozies Tool Kit (page 12)

3/4 yard (68.6 cm) of printed cotton fabric

3/4 yard (68.6 cm) of quilted cotton or flannel fabric for lining

11 inches (27.9 cm) each of three different 3/8-inch (9.5 mm) rickrack and ribbon trims

2 inches (5.1 cm) of 1/4-inch (6 mm) elastic

48 inches (121.9 cm) of 3/8 to 1/2-inch (9.5 mm to 1.3 cm) ribbon for ties

One 5/8 to 3/4-inch (1.6 to 1.9 cm) button

SEAM ALLOWANCE

1/4 inch (6 mm) unless otherwise noted

SIZE MATTERS

This cozy is designed to fit a 9 x 13-inch (22.9 x 33 cm) rectangular baking pan that is about 2 inches (5.1 cm) deep. If the pan you want to cover is a different size, adjust the project dimensions accordingly.

WHAT YOU DO

1 From both the printed fabric and the quilted lining, cut an 11 x 37 1/2-inch (27.9 x 95.3 cm) rectangle and a 15 x 25 1/2-inch (38.1 x 64.8 cm) rectangle. Use a teacup, ribbon spool, or other circular item to trace and cut rounded corners on both rectangles.

2 On the longer printed rectangle, pin the three 11- inch (27.9 cm) trim pieces on the right side of the fabric, 3 1/2 inches (8.9 cm) from one end. Baste at the ends and stitch across the trim 3 inches (7.6 cm) from each side (figure 1). Fold the 2-inch (5.1 cm) elastic piece in half, center the ends on the edge of the fabric, and baste.

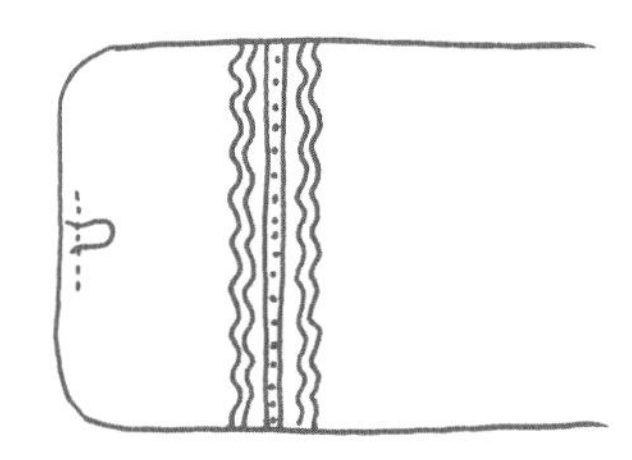

figure 1

(continued on next page)

A Sense of Direction

If your print is directional (the design has an obvious "up" and "down" direction), you will need more yardage of the printed fabric—1 1/8 yard (102.9 cm) instead of 3/4 yard (68.6 cm)—to cut it in the right direction. For the direction to be right side up on each cozy flap, do the following:

- Cut the printed fabric rectangles in step 1 an extra 1/2 inch (1.3 cm) longer (the width can remain the same).
- Cut both rectangles in half and turn one piece 180°. With right sides together, pin the fabrics and stitch them back together. When you open the fabric, the direction should be facing "up" on both sides of the seam.
- Press the seam open and round off the corners described in step 1.

3 With right sides together, pin the long fabric rectangle to the lining rectangle of the same size. Stitch all four edges, leaving a 5-inch (12.7 cm) opening along one side for turning. Trim the seams, turn right side out, and press. Do the same for the remaining small rectangles.

4 On the right (printed fabric) side of the short rectangle, mark where the ribbon ties will go. Measure 4 inches (10.2 cm) from each side and 2 inches (5.1 cm) from the end. Cut four pieces of ribbon 12 inches (30.5 cm) long. For each ribbon, fold under one end ½ inch (1.3 cm) and stitch the folded end to a mark (figure 2).

figure 2

5 With wrong sides facing up, center and pin the short rectangle on top of the long rectangle. Stitch around the edges of the short rectangle through all thicknesses. Turn the joined rectangles over and stitch around the edges of the long rectangle through all thicknesses.

6 Measure and mark 2¼ inches (5.7 cm) up from each corner as shown (figure 3). Bring right sides together at the marks and stitch.

7 Fit the pan into the cozy and close all the flaps. Mark the button placement under the elastic loop and hand sew the button in place. Time to bake some brownies.

figure 3

teapotcozy

After a brisk walk on a cold afternoon, it's so pleasant to go back to your nest, tuck your feet in warm slippers, and sip aromatic tea. Hold the heat in your teapot with a cozy that says home, sweet home.

DESIGNER

ANGELA COTTON

WHAT YOU NEED

- Basic Cozies Tool Kit (page 12)
- 7 x 15-inch (17.8 x 38.1 cm) piece of fabric for the cottage wall
- 6 x 15-inch (15.2 x 38.1 cm) piece of fabric for the cottage roof
- 12 x 15-inch (30.5 x 38.1 cm) square of batting
- 15-inch (38.1 cm) square of printed cotton for the lining
- Fabric scraps for door and window appliqués
- Fray retardant (optional)
- Basting glue (optional)
- 4 inches (10.2 cm) of 1/2-inch (1.3 cm) ribbon for the chimney tab

SEAM ALLOWANCE

3/8 inch (1 cm) unless otherwise noted

WHAT YOU DO

1 With right sides facing, pin one cottage wall piece to a cottage roof piece and stitch along one 15-inch (38.1 cm) side. Open the joined pieces and press flat with the seams pressed toward the roof piece. Do the same with the other two cottage pieces.

2 Enlarge the template on page 124. For each of the joined cottage pieces, lay the template on top, align the seam with the roof line, and cut out the house shape. Cut the bottom of the cozy where marked. Cut two batting pieces to the same size. Use the entire template shape to cut two lining pieces.

3 Using fabric scraps, cut a 2 x 2 3/4-inch (5 x 7 cm) rectangle for the door and four 1 1/2-inch (3.8 cm) squares for the windows. For all five pieces, trim the sides on a slight diagonal to echo the slant of the roof. Apply fray retardant, if desired, and allow the pieces to dry. Pin the appliqués to one of the cottage walls (or use basting glue) and then stitch in place.

4 Pin each batting piece to the back of each cottage piece and baste together with a 1/4-inch (6 mm) seam around the outermost edges.

5 Lay the cottage front right side up. Fold the 4-inch (10.2 cm) piece of ribbon in half lengthwise and pin the ends to the center of the front top edge (figure 1). Lay the other cottage piece on top, right side facing down. Stitch up one side, across the top, and down the other side. Trim the seam allowance as close as possible to the seam; trim the top corners at an angle (page 20), and turn the cozy right side out.

figure 1

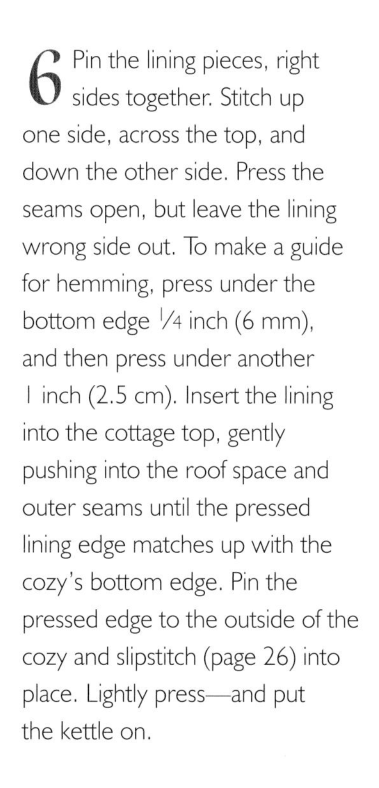

6 Pin the lining pieces, right sides together. Stitch up one side, across the top, and down the other side. Press the seams open, but leave the lining wrong side out. To make a guide for hemming, press under the bottom edge 1/4 inch (6 mm), and then press under another 1 inch (2.5 cm). Insert the lining into the cottage top, gently pushing into the roof space and outer seams until the pressed lining edge matches up with the cozy's bottom edge. Pin the pressed edge to the outside of the cozy and slipstitch (page 26) into place. Lightly press—and put the kettle on.

HOW BIG IS YOUR POT?

This project is designed to fit a 6-cup teapot about 6 inches (15.2 cm) high and 9 inches (22.9 cm) wide. There's quite a bit of leeway in this design, but if your teapot is significantly larger or smaller, adjust the template size before you cut. Remember to include seam allowances.

Weallscream

DESIGNER

KELLEY GRACE QUAKKELAAR

People who can't be bothered to scoop their dessert into a bowl—you know who you are, and there ain't no shame—will shout for joy. No more frozen fingertips! That problem solved, you can address more important issues: which flavor?

WHAT YOU NEED

Basic Cozies Tool Kit (page 12)

4 x 13½-inch (10.2 x 34.3 cm) piece of fabric

4½ x 13½-inch (11.4 x 34.3 cm) piece of fleece

SEAM ALLOWANCE

⅜ inch (9.5 mm) unless otherwise noted

WHAT YOU DO

1 With right sides together, line up the top edge of the fabric with the fleece, pin, and stitch.

2 Match up the bottom edges—the fleece will have a bump in it, since you want an edge of fleece showing along the top and bottom of the fabric when finished. Pin the pieces together so they don't shift, and stitch the bottom seam.

3 Turn the cozy right side out and press the edges lightly with an iron. Make sure you have an even border of fleece along the top and bottom of the fabric. Topstitch both edges.

4 Enlarge the template on page 128. Fold the cozy with right sides together and lay the template on top. Align the template "fold" edge with the folded cozy, and make sure the wider end matches up with the top of your fabric. Trace the pattern onto the fabric with chalk and stitch along that line. Trim the excess seam allowance, turn right side out, and head for the fridge.

tea party

DESIGNER

RACHEL E. DOWD

Slip a few teabags into a teeny appliquéd wallet, and you'll be ready to have tea for two at a moment's notice. Do you take sugar? Cream or lemon?

WHAT YOU NEED

- Basic Cozies Tool Kit (page 12)
- 4 x 12-inch (10.2 x 30.5 cm) piece of print fabric
- 2 x 3-inch (5.1 x 7.6 cm) scrap of the same print fabric
- Small pair of sharp scissors
- Fray retardant
- 4 x 12-inch (10.2 x 30.5 cm) piece of linen
- 18 inches (45.7 cm) of white embroidery floss
- 18 inches (45.7 cm) of silver metallic embroidery floss
- Embroidery needle
- 4 x 12-inch (10.2 x 30.5 cm) piece of fusible interfacing
- 1 snap and snap setting tool

SEAM ALLOWANCE

1/4 inch (6 mm) unless otherwise noted

WHAT YOU DO

1 Enlarge the template on page 120. Using a pencil, draw the teacup shape onto the wrong side of the fabric scrap. Cut out the outline with a small pair of sharp scissors. Don't cut out the handle hole yet. Apply fray retardant to all raw edges and allow it to dry.

2 At one short end of the linen piece, center the teacup shape about 1/2 to 3/4 inch (1.3 to 1.9 cm) from the edges and pin it in place. With a sewing machine or by hand, carefully stitch 1/8 inch (3 mm) from the edge all the way around the outline of the teacup and the handle, as indicated on the template. With the small scissors, carefully snip out the handle hole and apply fray retardant.

3 Using two strands of silver metallic embroidery floss with two strands of white, embroider "steam" swirls coming out the teacup in a running stitch (page 27).

4 Following the manufacturer's instructions, fuse the interfacing to the print fabric. On the right side of this piece, measure 1 inch (2.5 cm) from one of the short ends, find the midpoint from the sides, and mark the placement

(continued on next page)

of the snap. On the right side of the linen piece, measure 3 inches (7.6 cm) from the end opposite the embroidery, find the midpoint from the sides, and mark the placement of the other half of the snap.

5 Following the manufacturer's instructions, attach both halves of the snap on the right sides of the fabric as marked.

6 With right sides together, match the snap-end of the fabric piece to the teacup-end of the linen. Pin and stitch around the edges, leaving a 3-inch (7.6 cm) opening on one of the long sides for turning. Clip the four corners and turn the piece right side out through the opening. Carefully push out the corners, and press.

7 Fold the linen end with the snap (opposite the teacup end) to the inside 3¾ inches (9.5 cm) and pin. Fold the top flap over and check that the snaps align; then unfold it to lie flat. Starting at a bottom side, edgestitch up the side, across the top, and back down the other side to the bottom. Tuck in your favorite tea bags and slip the cozy into your purse.

Teatime is now anytime.

basket case

Breaking bread with friends and family? Keep baked goods warm with this nifty little treatment. All you need is a basket, your favorite fabric, and a little bit of dough for the craft store.

DESIGNER

JENNIFER WALLIN

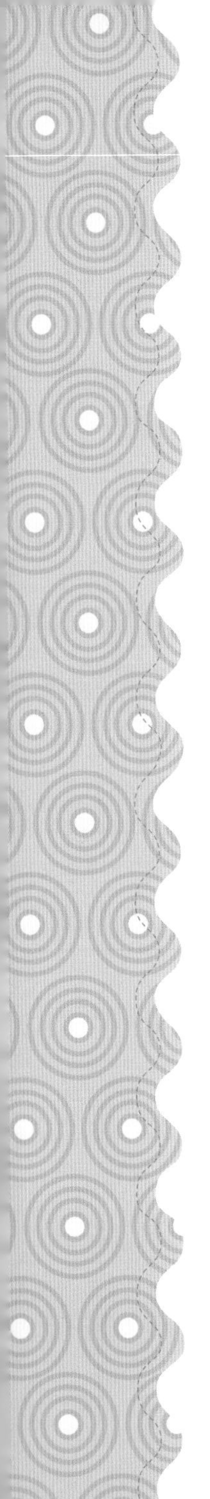

WHAT YOU NEED

Basic Cozies Tool Kit (page 12)

1 breadbasket

½ yard (45.7 cm) of main fabric

¼ yard (22.9 cm) of contrasting fabric

Enough ¼-inch (6 mm) elastic to encircle the breadbasket

3 yards (2.7 m) of twill tape

WHAT YOU DO

1 Measure the widest dimension of your breadbasket and add 4 inches (10.2 cm). Cut two rectangles from your main fabric at the above length and 8 inches (20.3 cm) wide. Cut two rectangles from the contrasting fabric at the same length and 4½ (11.4 cm) inches wide.

2 With right sides together, pin the length of a main fabric rectangle to a contrasting fabric rectangle and stitch. Press the seams towards the main fabric (figure 1). Repeat with the remaining rectangles. These pieces become the front and back of the cozy.

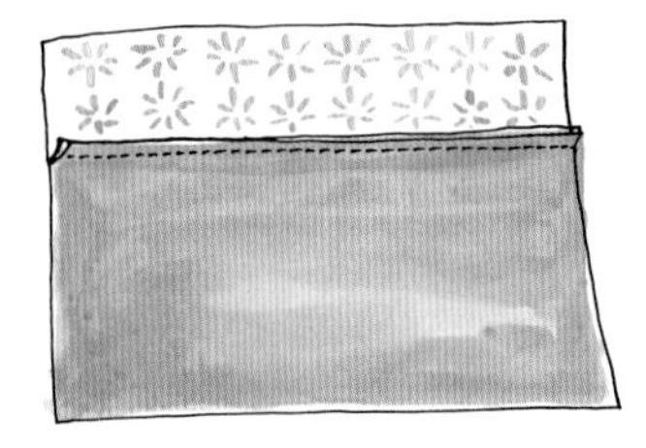

figure 1

3 With right sides facing, pin the front and back pieces together at the sides. On each side, measure 3 inches (7.6 cm) from the top of the contrasting fabric and mark the point with a pin or chalk. Stitch the seam from the bottom, stopping at the mark.

4 Press the side seams open, keeping the same width seam allowance for the unstitched sections. Stitch the folded seam allowance in place, turning the corner at the bottom of the V. Trim the seam allowance with pinking shears, if desired.

5 To make a casing (page 23) for the drawstring, press under the top edge of the fabric ¼ inch (6 mm). Press under again 1 inch (2.5 cm). Stitch the length of the folded edge (figure 2).

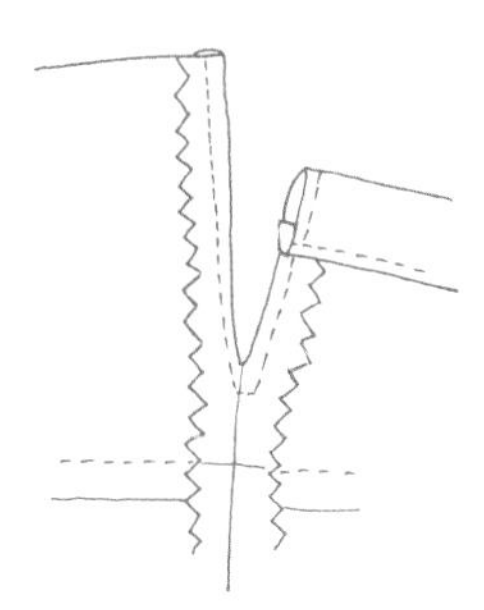

figure 2

6 Press under the bottom edge of the cozy 1/2 inch (1.3 cm) and baste. Cut the elastic (see the box on this page) and pin one end on the back of the basted seam. Loop the other end around (keeping the elastic untwisted), overlap the first end, and pin. Stitch the elastic in place, pulling it taut as you sew.

7 Cut the twill tape into two pieces that are each 54 inches (137.2 cm) long. Attach a safety pin to the end of one piece and guide it through the drawstring casing. Thread it all the way around the top, past the gap on the opposite side, and back where you started. Tie the ends together with a knot. Thread the other piece of twill tape from the opposite seam and knot it on that side.

8 Place the basket in the cozy with the elasticized edge on the bottom. Bring the cozy up over the sides of the basket and pull the knotted ends on both sides. The cozy will snug closed neatly and evenly.

Warm muffins, anyone?

GOOD STRETCH

The elastic at the bottom of the cozy helps keep it in place on the breadbasket. For elastic that is not too loose or too tight, try this:

1. Measure the distance around the breadbasket.

2. Divide that number by 4.

3. Subtract the answer in step 2 from the distance measured in step 1. Cut your elastic to this length.

egg cap

Keep your hard-boiled egg warm with a fanciful topper shaped like a house. The casually appliquéd windows and doors add dashes of charm and emphasize the color of the red roof.

DESIGNER

ANGELA COTTON

WHAT YOU NEED

- Basic Cozies Tool Kit (page 12)
- 3 x 5-inch (7.6 x 12.7 cm) fabric scrap for the cottage wall
- 4 x 5-inch (10.2 x 12.7 cm) fabric scrap for the cottage roof
- 6-inch (15.2 cm) square of printed cotton for the lining
- Fabric scraps for door and window appliqués
- Fray retardant (optional)
- Basting glue
- 2 inches (5.1cm) of ½-inch (1.3 cm) ribbon for the chimney tab

SEAM ALLOWANCE

Seam allowance ⅜ inch (9.5 mm) unless otherwise noted

WHAT YOU DO

1 With right sides facing, pin one cottage wall piece to a cottage roof piece and stitch along one 5-inch (12.7 cm) side. Open the joined pieces and press flat with the seams pressed toward the roof piece. Do the same with the other two cottage pieces.

2 Enlarge the template on page 124. For both joined cottage pieces, lay the template on top, align the seam with the roof line, and cut out the house shape. Cut the bottom of the cozy where marked. Use the entire template shape to cut two lining pieces.

3 From fabric scraps, cut a ¾ x 1½-inch (1.9 x 3.8 cm) rectangle for the door and four ¾-inch (1.9 cm) squares for the windows. For all five pieces, trim the sides on a slight diagonal to echo the slant of the roof. Apply fray retardant, if desired, and allow the pieces to dry. Use basting glue to position the appliqués to one of the cottage walls and then stitch in place.

4 Lay the cottage front right side up. Fold the 2-inch (5.1 cm) piece of ribbon in half lengthwise, and pin the ends to the center of the front top edge (figure 1). Lay the other cottage piece on top, right side facing down. Stitch up one side, across the top, and down the other side. Trim the seam allowance, cut the top corners at an angle (page 20), and turn the cozy right side out.

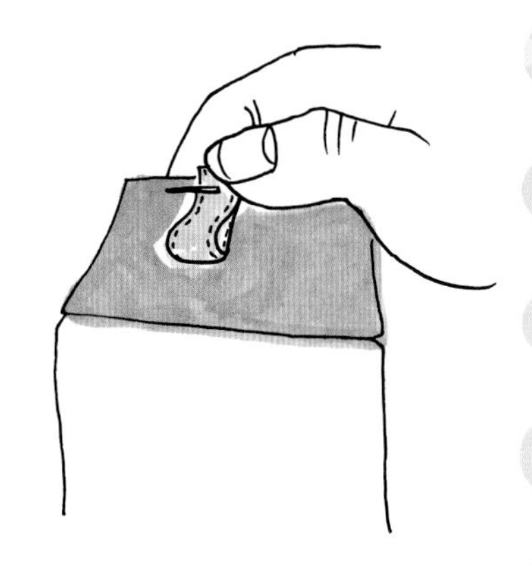

figure 1

5 Pin the lining pieces, right sides together. Stitch up one side, across the top, and down the other side. Press the seams open, but leave the lining wrong side out. To make a guide for hemming, press under the bottom edge ¼ inch (6 mm), and then press under another ⅜ inch (9.5 mm). Insert the lining into the cottage top, gently pushing into the roof space and outer seams until the pressed lining edge matches up with the cozy's bottom edge. Pin the pressed edge to the outside of the cozy and slipstitch (page 26) into place. Lightly press.

coffee cup quilt

Go green while keeping your fingers safe from burns by bringing your own cup cozy when you get joe to go. Everyone will wonder where that funky java joint is.

DESIGNER

ALYSSE HENNESSEY

WHAT YOU NEED

Basic Cozies Tool Kit (page 12)

5 x 12-inch (12.7 x 30.5 cm) piece of background fabric

5 x 12-inch (12.7 x 30.5 cm) piece of fleece

Scraps of fabric, rickrack, and ribbon

WHAT YOU DO

1 Enlarge the template on page 121, and set it aside.

2 Look through your stash for fabric printed with cute images that are less than 2½ inches (6.4 cm) in size. Now is their chance to shine. Pull out a couple of your favorites, with some background fabrics to match.

3 Lay the fleece right side down with the background fabric on top, right side up. Lay the enlarged template on top, and trace the template onto the fabric with chalk or a marker. Leave yourself at least an inch outside the template on all sides.

4 Using either matching or contrasting thread, stitch randomly back and forth a few times with a long straight stitch, both inside and outside the boundaries of the template outline (figure 1). Don't use short stitches as they can cause the top fabric to migrate.

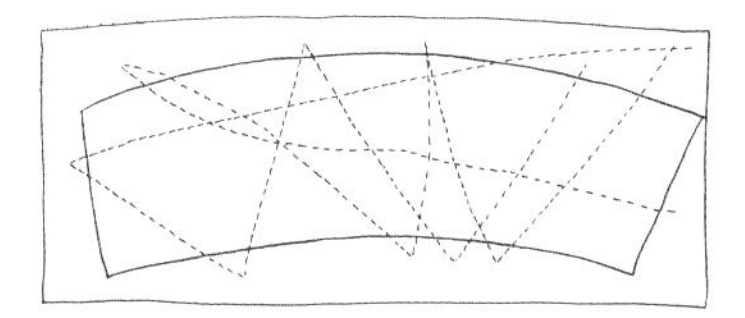

figure 1

5 Cut an image or two from the printed fabrics and arrange them on the cozy, making them longer than the template tracing (figure 2). Add strips of accent fabrics, rickrack, or ribbon. Pin them all in place.

figure 2

6 Using variegated threads or contrasting colors, stitch over the raw edges using a medium-wide zigzag or buttonhole stitch. Don't make the stitches too narrow, or the raw edges will pull out when used. Does your machine have fancy stitches? Now is a good time to use them in the open spaces.

7 Cut out the cozy on the marked template lines. Stitch the top and bottom edges with a wide zigzag, very close to the edge. When the needle falls just off the fabric on the right, the stitch will effectively wrap the raw edges.

8 With right sides together, stitch the ends with a medium-length straight stitch, backstitching at both ends.

Turn the cozy right side out, snug it over a cup, and you're ready to pour.

sunny side up

You could just grab the griddle handle with a rag, but you've got more flair than that. Cover it with this cute cozy and you're ready to serve 'em up hot.

DESIGNER

LISA MACCHIA

WHAT YOU NEED

Basic Cozies Tool Kit (page 12)
1/8 yard (11.4 cm) of fabric
8 x 10-inch (20.3 x 25.4 cm) piece of felt, any color
Small pieces of white and yellow felt
Black and pink cotton embroidery thread

How Big Is Your Panhandle?
The template in this book won't fit all panhandles. Before cutting your fabric, check the template against the handle you want to cover. Remember to allow for the 1/2-inch (1.3 cm) seam on all sides. You also need some wiggle room for the thickness of the handle. If the cozy isn't large enough, add what you need to the template outline.

SEAM ALLOWANCE

1/4 inch (6 mm) unless otherwise noted

WHAT YOU DO

1 Enlarge the template on page 120. Cut out two pieces of fabric and two pieces of felt for the front and back of your panhandle cozy. From the smaller pieces, cut out the egg white and yolk shapes.

2 Pin the egg white at the bottom and widest point of the panhandle, about 1/2 inch (1.3 cm) away from the edges (to allow for seams). Stitch all around the outer edge (figure 1). Stitch the yolk in the center of the white.

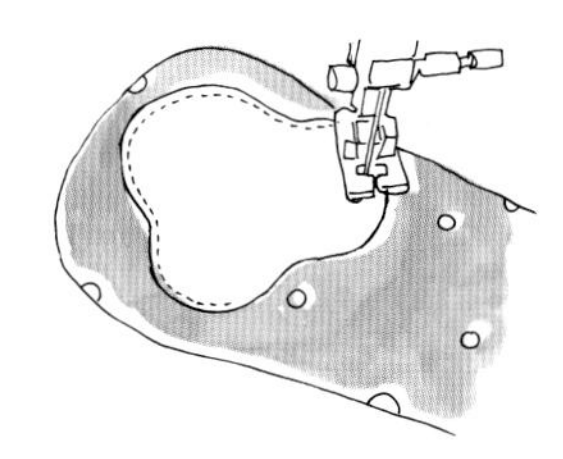

figure 1

(continued on next page)

3 Use an embroidery needle and black embroidery thread to stitch two Xs for the eyes. Use pink thread to stitch a mouth. To make the egg smile, secure the center of the mouth line with another stitch. Tie and knot off all thread ends.

4 Pin the right side of one fabric piece to a felt piece. Stitch them together at the narrowest end only (figure 2). Flip the fabric over so the right side faces out. Do the same for the remaining fabric piece and felt piece.

figure 2

5 Pin the paired pieces together with the fabric right sides together. (The felt will be on the top and bottom.) Leaving the top open, stitch down one side and around to the other side (figure 3). Trim the seam allowance very close to the seam.

6 Turn the cozy inside out to reveal the right side of the fabric and egg appliqué. Because the layers are thick, you may need to coax the cozy a bit to get it turned. Press out any wrinkles, dress up your panhandle, and get cooking!

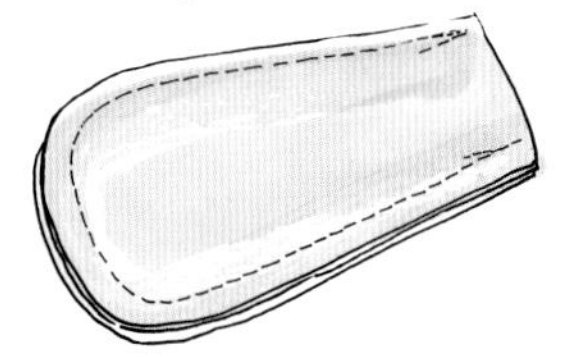

figure 3

press on

Cold coffee—ick! Wrap this whimsical patchworked cozy around your French press to keep the fresh java piping hot and your morning good.

DESIGNER

LAURRAINE YUYAMA

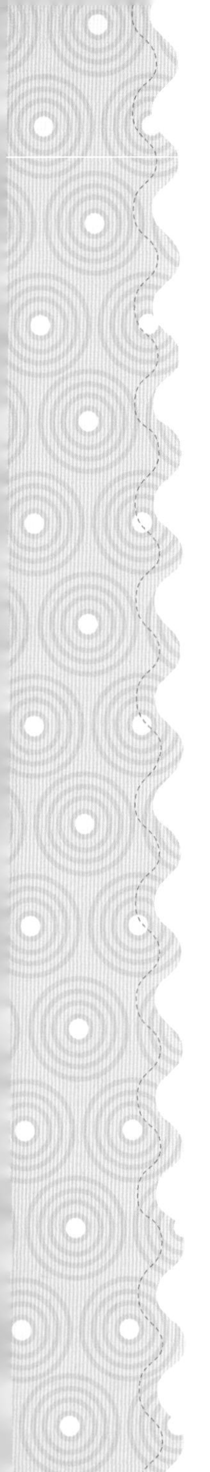

WHAT YOU NEED

Basic Cozies Tool Kit (page 12)

5 coordinating fabric scraps for the background

12 x 15-inch (30.5 x 38.1 cm) piece of striped fabric for binding, ties, and the knob

Scraps of lightweight fusible web

Various fabric scraps for the appliqués

Scraps of felt for the leaf appliqués (different shades of green if possible)

9 x 16-inch (22.9 x 40.6 cm) piece of needle-punched batting*

9 x 16-inch (22.9 x 40.6 cm) piece of high-loft polyester batting

9 x 16-inch (22.9 x 40.6 cm) piece of fabric for backing

Embroidery thread in a variety of colors

9 buttons in a variety of sizes

12 inches (30.5 cm) of thin elastic cord

* *During the manufacture of needle-punched batting, needles poke the fibers over and over, causing them to tangle together and become tightly interwoven. This creates more density, making needle-punched batting firmer, heavier, and therefore better able to retain heat than bonded battings.*

SEAM ALLOWANCE

$\frac{1}{4}$ inch (6 mm) unless otherwise noted

Fitting Info

- *This pattern fits a press 7 inches (17.8 cm) tall and 12 inches (30.5 cm) around. Since the cozy is just a flat rectangle with ties, it's easy to alter the dimensions to fit your press.*

WHAT YOU DO

1 Enlarge the templates on pages 126-127, and cut the pieces as follows:

- Cut the background fabrics to the sizes listed below:

Rectangle 1 = $3\frac{1}{2}$ x $6\frac{3}{4}$ inches (8.9 x 17.1 cm)

Rectangle 2 = $3\frac{1}{2}$ x 4 inches (8.9 x 10.2 cm)

Rectangle 3 = $3\frac{1}{2}$ x $10\frac{1}{4}$ inches (8.9 x 26 cm)

Rectangle 4 = 6 x $6\frac{1}{2}$ inches (15.2 x 16.5 cm)

Rectangle 5 = $2\frac{1}{4}$ x $15\frac{1}{2}$ inches (5.7 x 39.4 cm)

- Cut two 2 x 15-inch (5.1 x 38.1 cm) binding strips across the width of the striped fabric. Cut six $1\frac{1}{2}$ x 7-inch (3.8 x 17.8 cm) ties with the stripes running lengthwise. Cut two circles for the knob cozy.

- On the paper side of the fusible web, trace the appliqué pieces, leaving $\frac{1}{2}$ inch (1.3 cm) between them: three flower pots of different lengths, three flowerpot tops, and the butterfly wings and body. Cut out the shapes, leaving space outside the lines. Following the manufacturer's instructions, fuse them to the wrong side of the chosen fabrics and let them cool. Cut out the shapes on the drawn lines and leave the paper backings in place for now.

- For the five-petal flowers, cut two circles from the same fabric for each flower (total of four circles). Transfer the dots to the right side of the fabric.

- Cut two yo-yo flower circles from two different fabrics.

- Cut nine leaf shapes from the felt scraps.

2 To make the five-petal flowers, match two circles with right sides together and stitch around the entire edge. Cut notches in the seam allowance. Cut a small slit in the center of one side, turn right side out, and press. With doubled thread, hand sew up through the center of the circle and back down; come up through the dot and back down through the center. Pull tight. Repeat through each dot, finishing up in the center. Make two.

3 Make two yo-yo flowers (page 25) and six ties (page 23).

4 Assemble the background by pinning rectangles 1 and 2 on the sides, right sides together. Stitch and press the seams open. Pin these to rectangle 3 on the long side; stitch and press. Stitch this block to rectangle 4 and press. Finish by stitching the pieced block to rectangle 5. Press all seams flat. Aligning the seams, trace the template shape onto the pieced background and cut it out. (If your background fabrics are light enough, you can slip the template under the background and see it well enough to trace the design with a pencil. A lighttable makes this a cinch.)

5 Arrange the appliqué pieces on the background, aligning the bottom edge of the flowerpots to the bottom edge of the background. Following the manufacturer's instructions, peel off the paper backings and fuse the pieces in place.

(continued on next page)

6 Lay the polyester batting out flat, and lay the needle-punched batting on top of it. Lay the backing right side up over the batting. Center the pieced background face down on top of the backing, leaving space above and below. Pin and stitch both short sides, trimming the excess batting and backing from the sewn edge (figure 1). Save the batting scraps for the knob cozy. Turn the cozy right side out and facing up. Press the sewn edges flat.

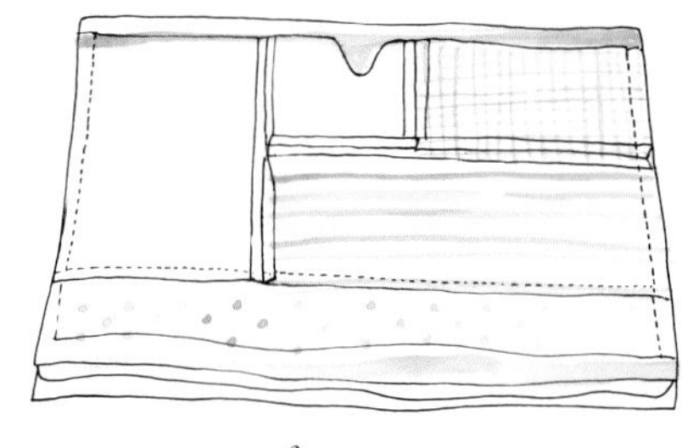

figure 1

7 Stitch around the flowerpot appliqué shapes, using a blanket stitch if available on your machine. Run a straight stitch along all visible background seams, without stitching through any appliqués. Stitch around the butterfly wings twice and use a blanket stitch or zigzag around the edge of the body.

8 With right sides together, align the long binding strips with the top and bottom edges of the background. Pin in place, turning under the ends to align with the edge (figure 2). Trim the excess batting. Fold the binding strip over to the back, turn the fabric under, and whipstitch in place.

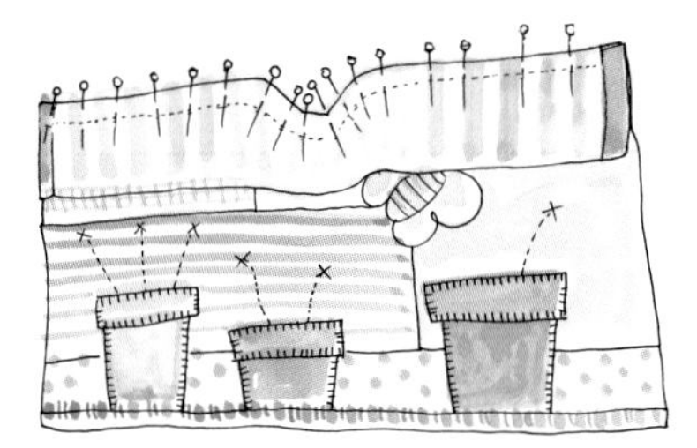

figure 2

9 Stitch and embroider the design elements. Use a running stitch (page 27) to trace the butterfly trails. Sew antennae using a backstitch (page 27) or double running stitch with a French knot at the ends. Sew an X on the bottom of each butterfly wing. Use a backstitch or double running stitch to sew stems for the flowers. Attach the felt leaves with a line of stitching down each center. Position each flower, add a button on top, and stitch it in place. (Two of the flowers consist of only a button.) Stitch matching buttons to the top butterfly wings.

10 Position and pin the ties in place, about 1/2 inch (1.3 cm) from the edge. Stitch a small square to secure.

11 To make the knob cozy (figure 3), pin the circles right sides together and stitch, leaving an opening where marked. Turn right side out and press. Stitch a 3/8-inch (9.5 mm) channel around the edge, leaving an opening in the same spot. Fluff up some leftover high-loft batting and push it through the hole into the center (don't overfill). Machine stitch the inner opening closed and thread the elastic cord through the channel. Position the cozy over the knob to check how tight to pull the elastic cord—enough to hold the cozy in place, but loose enough to be removed. Knot the elastic and whipstitch the opening closed.

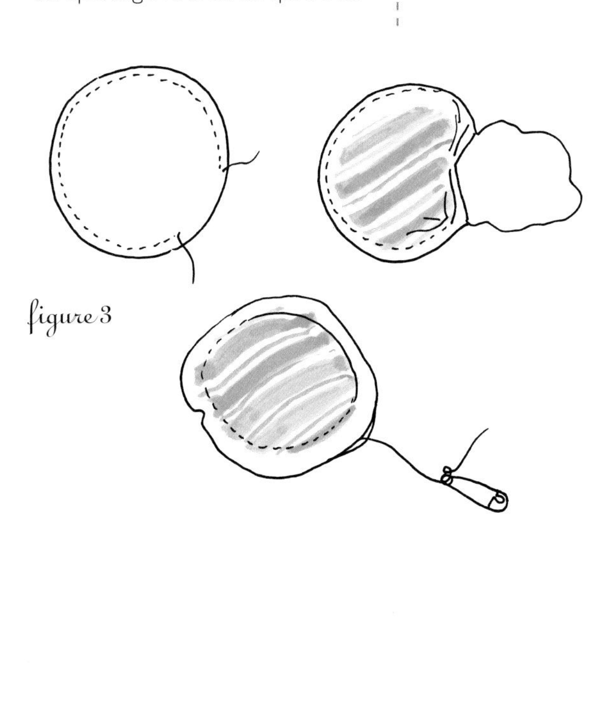

figure 3

templates

scanner manner
page 84
enlarge 400%

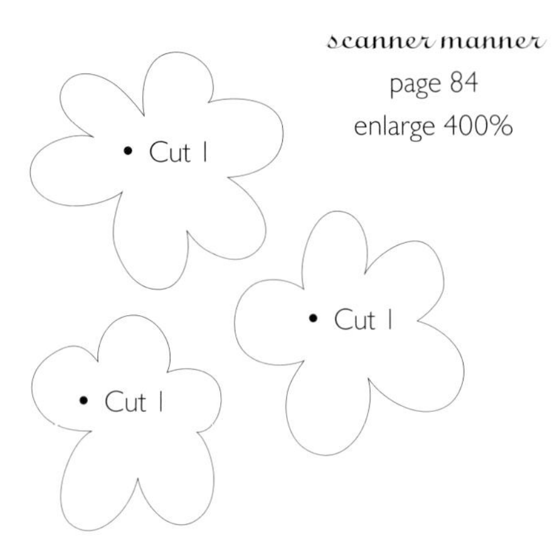

sunny side up
page 112
enlarge 200%

Front and Back

• Cut 2 fabric
• Cut 2 felt

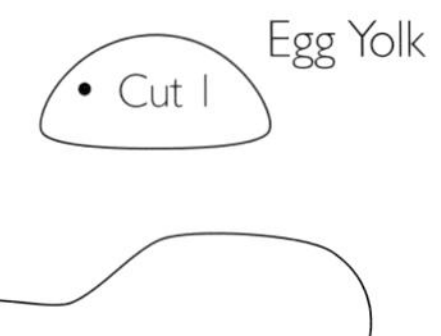

Egg White
• Cut 1

tea party
page 102
enlarge 100%

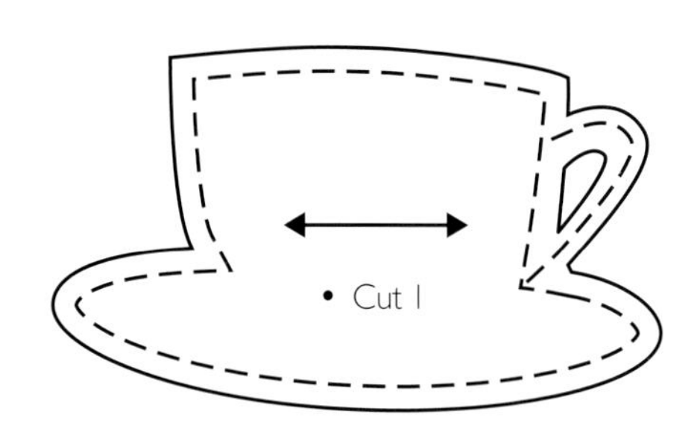

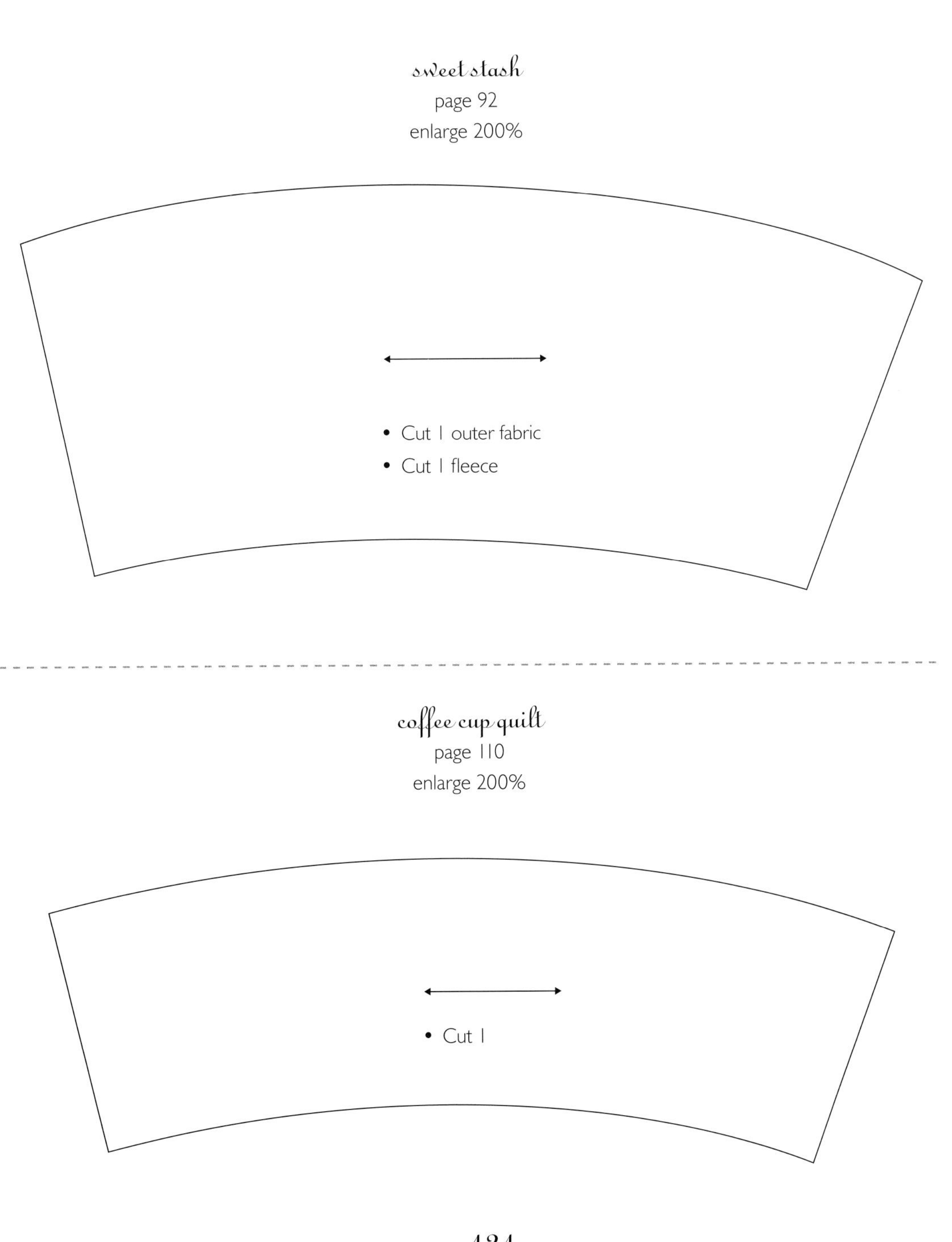
sweet stash
page 92
enlarge 200%
• Cut 1 outer fabric
• Cut 1 fleece
coffee cup quilt
page 110
enlarge 200%
• Cut 1

lip service

page 30

enlarge 400%

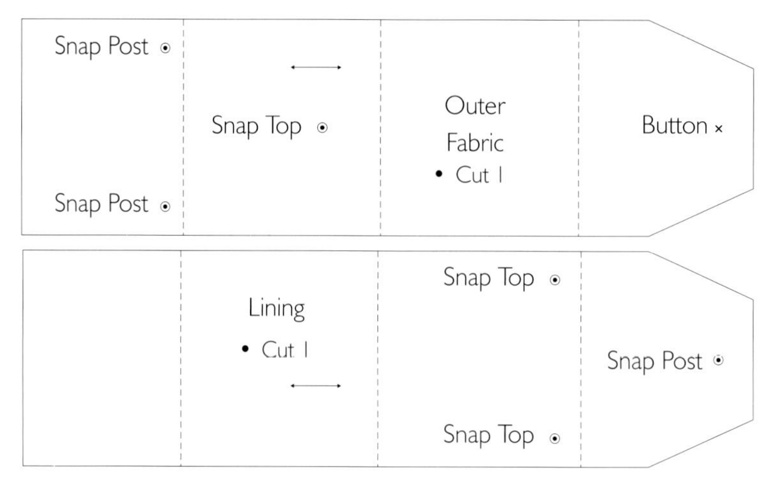

card cache

page 34

enlarge 200%

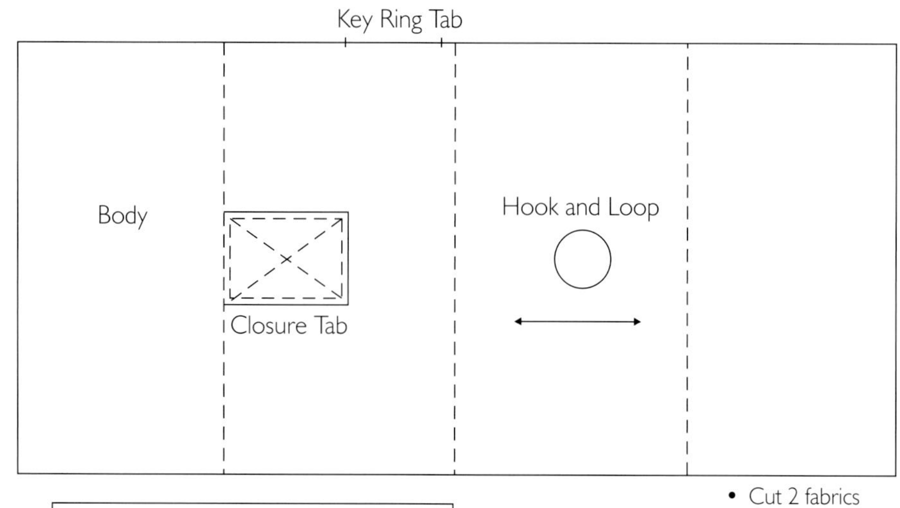

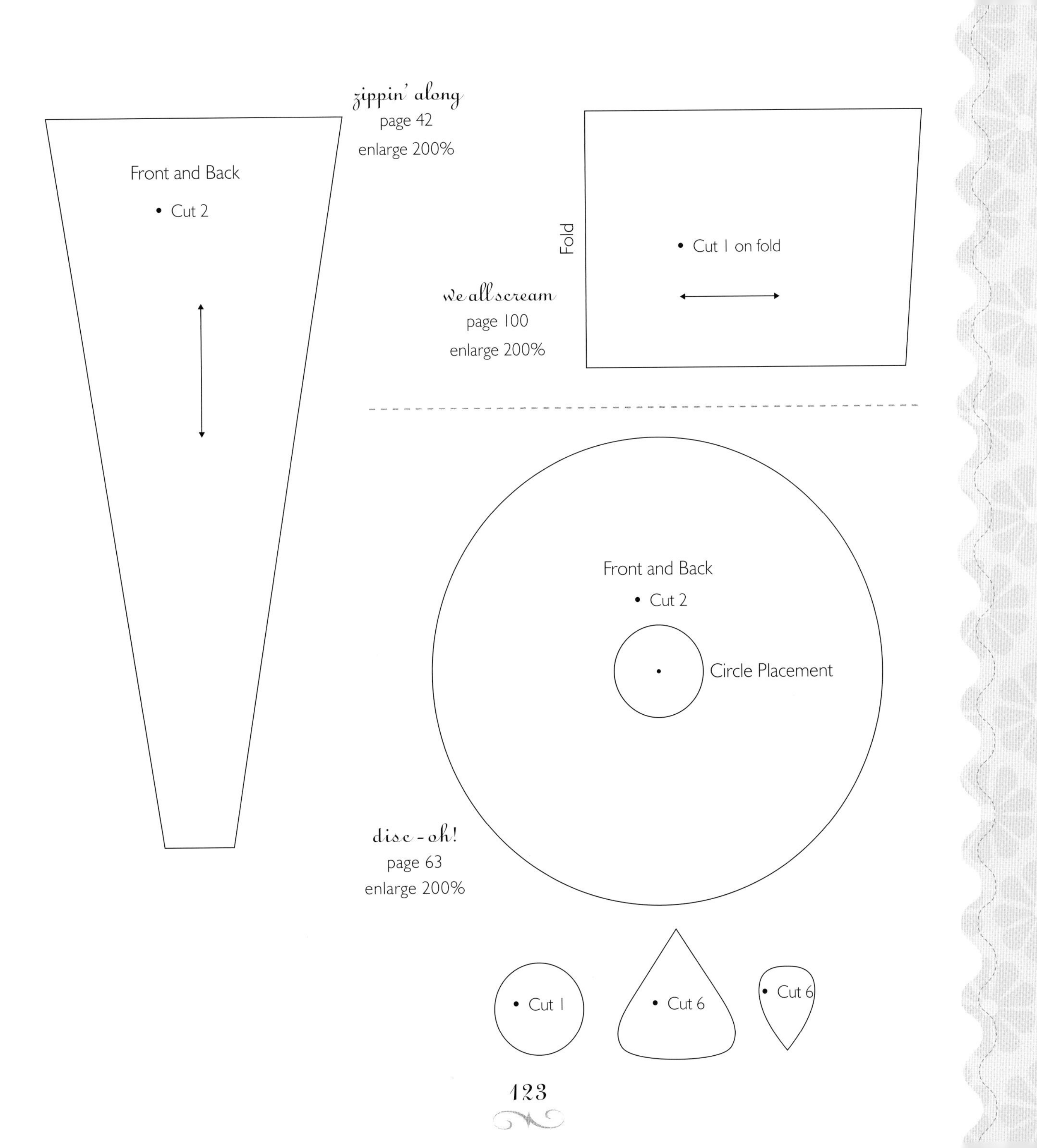
zippin' along
page 42
enlarge 200%
Front and Back
• Cut 2
Fold
• Cut 1 on fold
we all scream
page 100
enlarge 200%
Front and Back
• Cut 2
Circle Placement
disc-oh!
page 63
enlarge 200%
• Cut 1
• Cut 6
• Cut 6

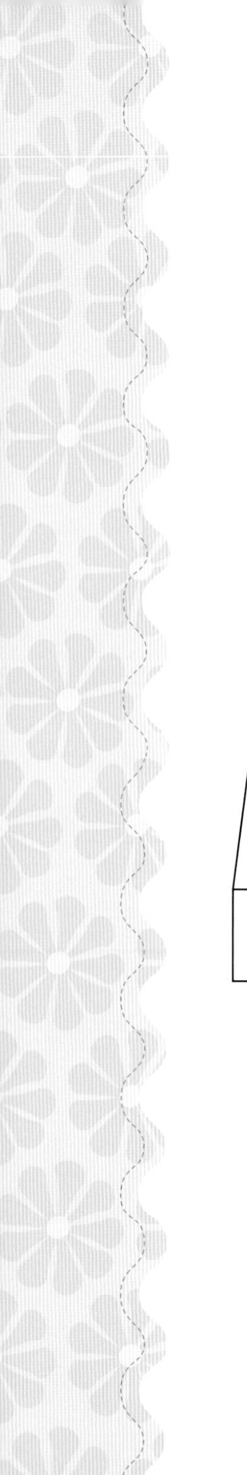

teapot cozy

page 97

enlarge 400%

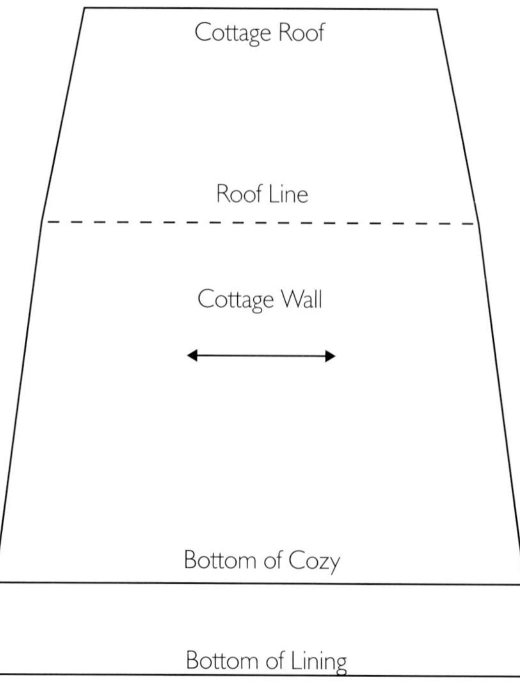

egg cap

page 108

enlarge 200%

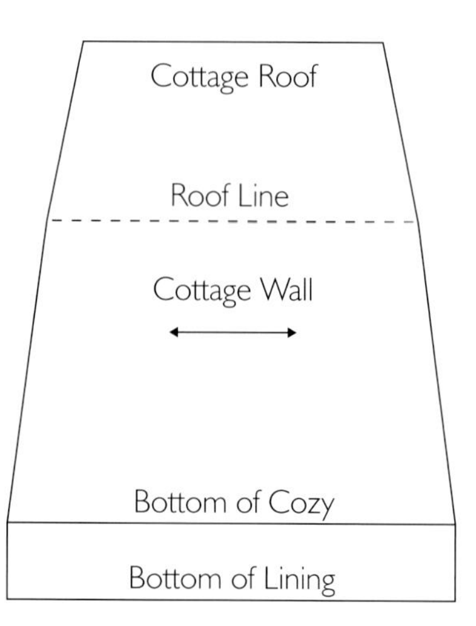

you rang?
page 71
enlarge 400%

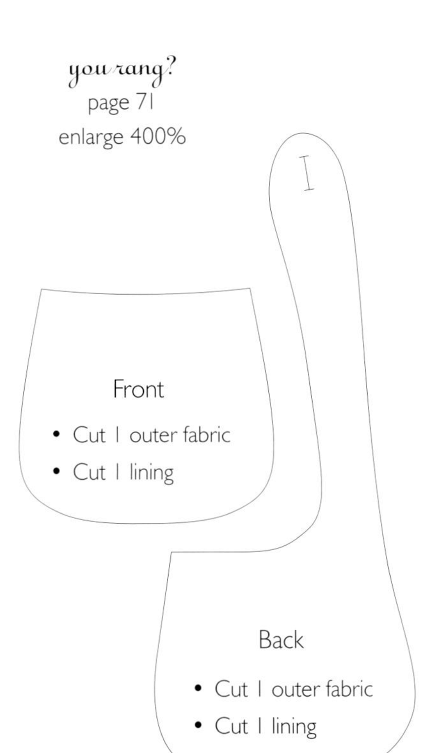

picture perfect
page 77
enlarge 200%

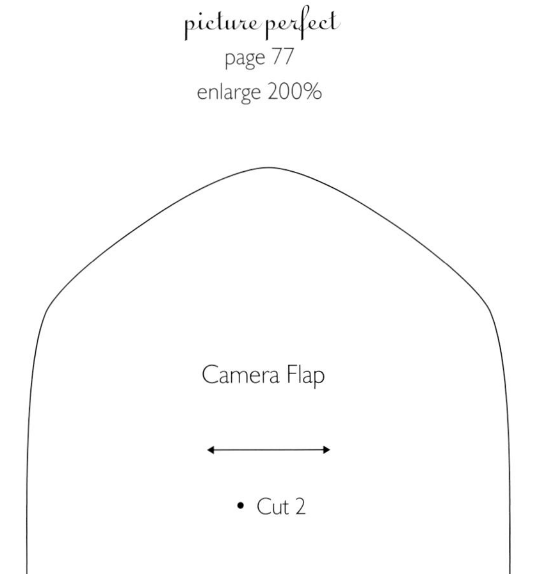

press on

page 115

enlarge 200%

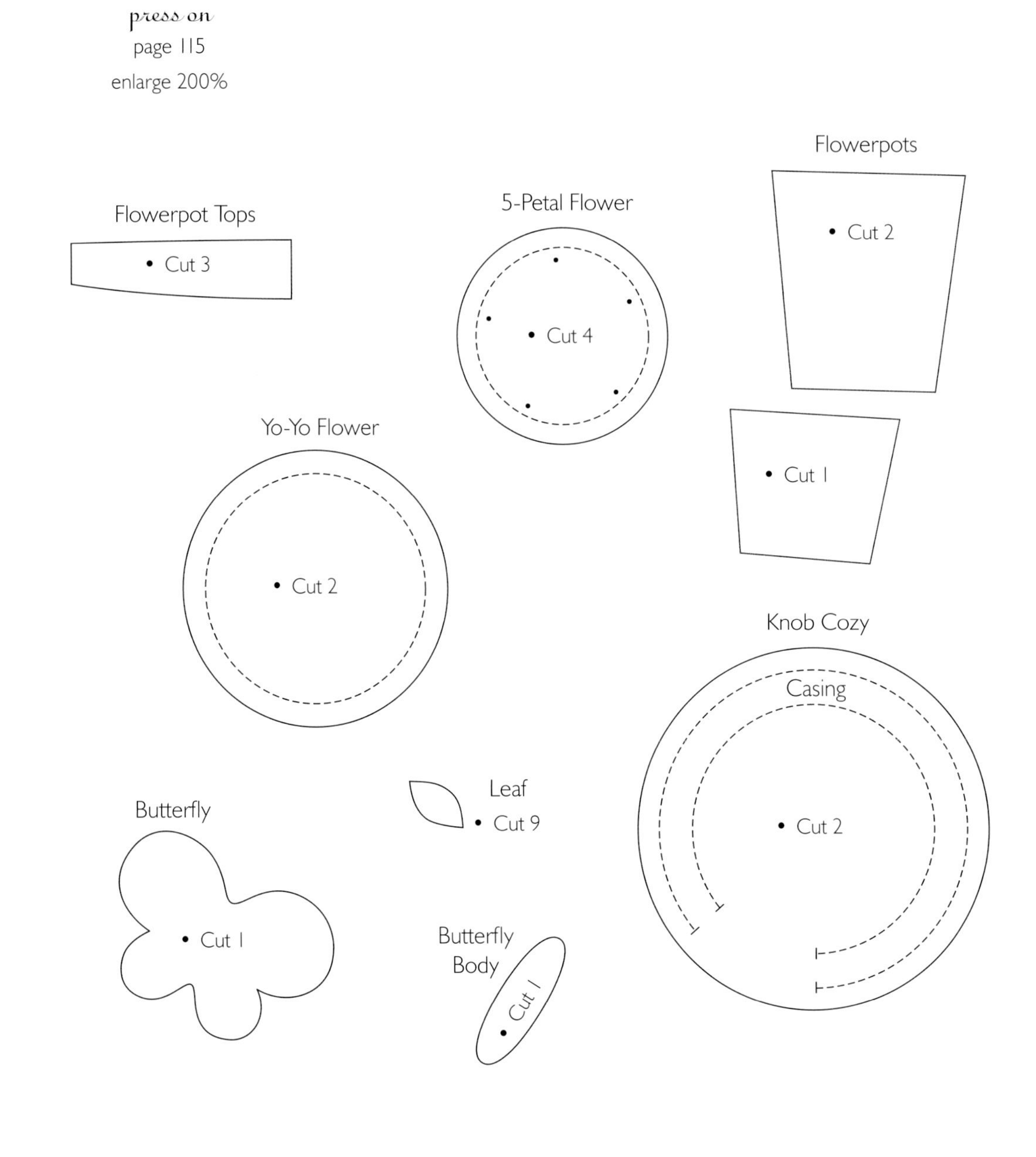

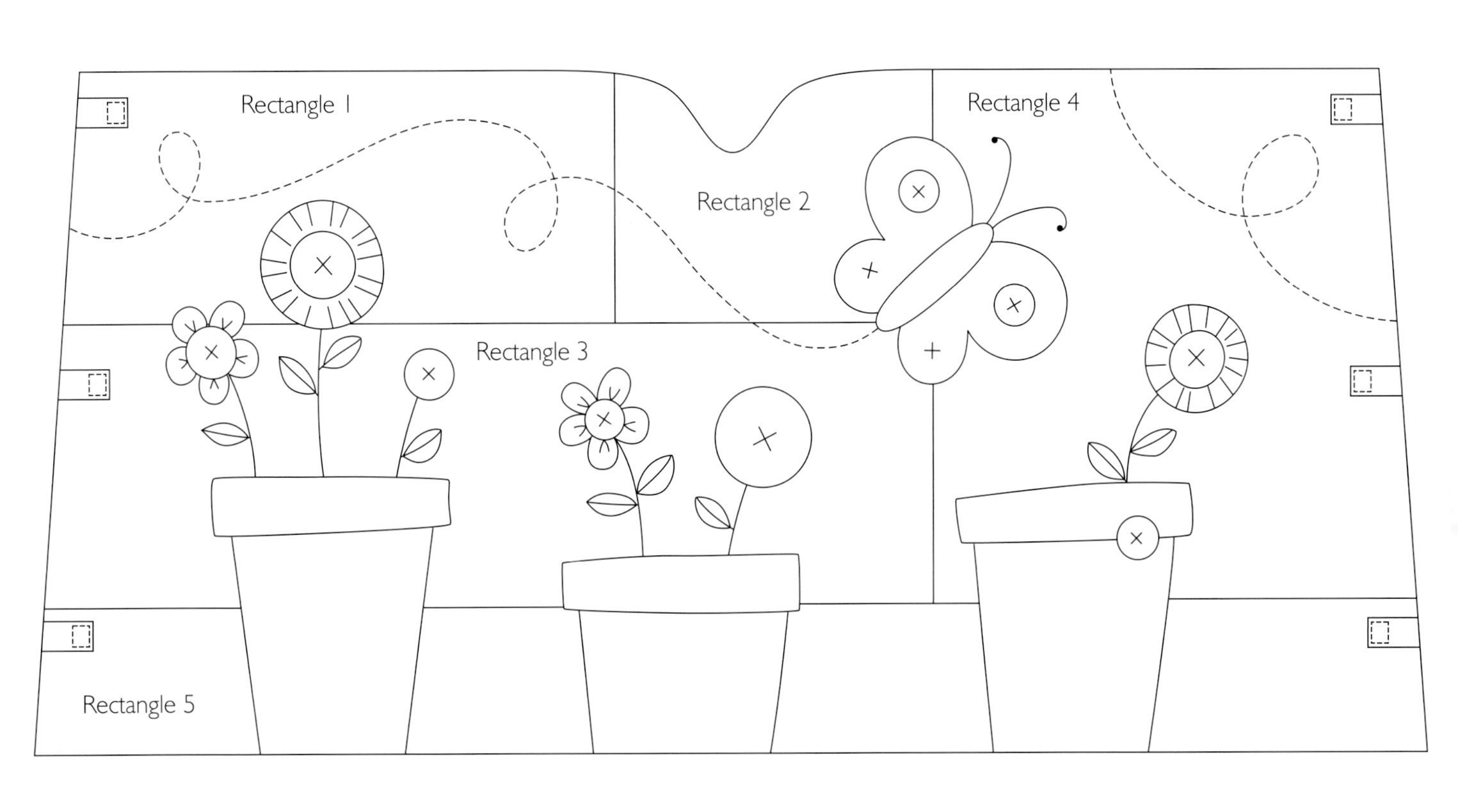
Rectangle 1
Rectangle 2
Rectangle 4
Rectangle 3
Rectangle 5

about the designers

TAYLOR ANDERSON is 15 and has spent half of her life growing up in Japan among the cherry blossoms and golden beaches. In 2002, she flew across the world to her new home in southern Oregon, where she currently resides with her parents, brother, sister, two dogs, a cat, and a fish. Creating beauty, whether through music or crafting, has always been a part of her life. In her free time between school and rehearsals, she can be found playing the violin, hanging out with friends, or working on her latest crafting endeavor.

HELEN ANGHARAD HENLEY was born and bred in Wales. She now lives with her husband and two children in the South of England. Helen holds an Oxford degree. Following a short period as a part-time university lecturer and research assistant, she left academia to become a full-time mother to her four-year-old daughter and two-year old son. After receiving a sewing machine for her thirtieth birthday and discovering the wide world of crafting blogs, she was inspired to set up an etsy shop (www.angharad.etsy.com) selling bags, baby bibs, quilts, and other handmade items. Helen also recently started a sewing and knitting blog that you can view at angharadhandmade.blogspot.com.

ROBIN BEAVER'S mother and grandmother inspired a love of needlecraft in her when she was young, and ever since it has served as a great source of creativity, satisfaction, and peace in her life. She enjoys making all types of clothing from christening gowns to wedding dresses, and everything in between. Outside of crafting, Robin is kept busy as an Instructional Technology Specialist, an adjunct college professor, Sunday school coordinator, and member of the Board of Trustees for her local library. She has two handsome and talented sons at college, and enjoys spending time with her family. See her work at fibergarden.etsy.com.

ANGELA COTTON lives in rural Shropshire, England. After completing a BA (Hons) Design degree, she worked as a freelance designer until starting her own business, Cotton Bird Designs. Angela makes one-of-a-kind, hand-stitched sculptures using mostly vintage paper and fabrics. She takes inspiration from old linens and cottons, animals, architecture, and nature. To add her own special touch, she stitches mainly by hand. Before beginning a new project, Angela creates mood boards in the form of little arrangements that sit on her tables, chairs, and shelves. Currently, Angela is working on stitched illustrations and sculptures. To discuss commissions or see more work, please visit www.cottonbird.co.uk.

RACHEL E. DOWD is a stay-at-home mom who has pursued many forms of arts and crafts since she was a little girl, including painting, sewing, dressmaking, embroidery, and mural painting. She just recently started designing and selling handbags, totes, accessories, baby quilts, and more in her online shops, ohsewfresh.etsy.com and ohsewfreshbaby.etsy.com. Rachel loves the familiarity and nostalgia that comes from combining vintage fabrics with modern designs. She lives in Dayton, Ohio, with her husband and their two-year-old daughter. She can be contacted at ohsewfresh@gmail.com

CHEYENNE GOH has always been making things. Along the way, she got a degree in biology, worked as a video producer, and then as a journalist. She lives in Vancouver, which is where she sits now, crafting and dreaming up new ways of recycling wearables and other bits and bobs. Check out her online store at www.RumahKampung.etsy.com.

MARIA GORETTI YEN is an artist and crafter who is still trying to decide what she wants to be when she grows up. She has a B.S. in Sociology, as well as a Juris Doctorate. Maria spends most of her days experimenting with sewing, painting, sculpting, drawing, and pottery throwing. See Maria's accessories at GreedyGoretti.etsy.com, and her Blythe doll boutique at LambySnow.etsy.com. Maria can be contacted at greedygoretti@yahoo.com.

WENDI GRATZ lives in Bakersville, North Carolina, with her family and her sewing machine. In school, she skipped home ec in favor of wood and metal shop, and didn't learn to use a sewing machine until she was in college. Her first project was a badly made tablecloth. Now she makes fun clothes, funky dolls, and all kinds of quilts. Visit www.wendigratz.com for more information.

ALYSSE HENNESSEY lives in Eugene, Oregon, with her partner, two brilliant young sons, a chocolate lab, and two sassy hens. She is a full-time artist and creates functional pieces out of both new and up-cycled materials. You can contact Alysse at alyssehennessey@gmail.com or see what's hoppin' in her Bliss Monkey etsy store, AlyTheRed.etsy.com.

SARAH LALONE lives and works as a student and independent designer in Ontario, Canada, with her husband and son. She created Punchanella in 2007 to share her creations with the rest of the world. Her items range from tote bags to purse accessories and home furnishings. You can see Sarah's blog and shop at www.punchanella.com.

MEREDITH GALLOWAY Kistner loves tooling around in her golf cart; hanging out with her husband, Rich, and their seven wiener dogs; and surprising friends with spontaneous visits. She's a gymnastics coach with an appreciation for dueling pianos, etsy, and cheese of any kind. Drop her a line at meratthelake@aol.com.

LISA MACCHIA is the designer and owner of Ity-Bity Bags. She takes inspiration from fairy tales, daydreams, and nostalgic memories. Lisa enjoys using different materials and techniques in her projects and is always open to trying something new. Her creations are playful, colorful, and full of whimsy. See for yourself at www.itybitybags.etsy.com.

BETHANY MANN is a seamstress, stylist, and mom, who resides in the Santa Cruz Mountains in California with her husband, son, and a couple of cats. She sews clothes from vintage patterns for herself and makes jewelry, toys, and aprons for her etsy store. She has appeared in other Lark books in this series, including *Pretty Little Patchwork* (2007) and *Pretty Little Potholders* (2007). Any free time she has is spent in thrift stores and flea markets, looking for alternative crafting materials and colorful anecdotes for her blog bitterbettyindustries.blogspot.com.

MORGAN MOORE is a mother, artist, and self-admitted fabric junkie. Most days you'll find her whipping up delicious treats in her kitchen or designing new products for her online shop. She's based out of Los Angeles, California, and lives with her husband, Chris, and two children. Visit Morgan and check out her blog at http://morganmoore.typepad.com.

JOAN K. MORRIS'S artistic endeavors have led her down many successful creative paths, including ceramics and costume design for motion pictures. Joan has contributed projects for numerous Lark books, including *Hardware Style* (2004), *The Beaded Home* (2002), *Fun & Fabulous Pillows to Sew* (2006), *Button! Button!* (2008), and many more.

STACEY MURRAY is the name behind the Sheeps Clothing range of pure wool hand knitted hats, scarves, and hair accessories. She comes from a long line of knitters and began experimenting with beanies and scarves. When not knitting, blogging, sweeping the floor, or picking up toys, Stacey enjoys sewing. Having given up on making her own clothes due to constant mishaps (putting the scissors through a dress she had stayed up all night finishing before a wedding being one such example), Stacey now prefers to sew little bits and pieces such as tea cozies, handkerchief pouches, and lipstick cozies. For more information, please visit www.sheepsclothing.com.au and www.sheepsclothing.blogspot.com.

KELLEY GRACE QUAKKELAAR is the designer and owner of Gracie Designs. She has been married for five years to Dean, and they live in De Pere, Wisconsin. Family is very important to her and she tests everything on them. She has been crafting ever since she can remember, and has an addiction to all things cute. Nowadays, her designs include coffee and ice cream cuddlers, headbands, button-fancy barrettes, and jewelry. Her tagline is "Be Cute Now." You can find Kelley, and her goodies, at http://ShopGracieDesigns.com.

JULIE ROMINE lives on a small ranch in Kansas with her husband, two young boys, and a new baby girl. Whenever time permits, she draws patterns from the ideas that swirl in her head and makes her creations come to life. Julie learned to sew from her mother, JoAnn. Julie enjoys all kinds of crafting, from sculpting polymer clay fairies to hand embroidering onesies, but her favorite pastime is sewing and inventing new things. Find her creations online at www.blueberrymama.etsy.com.

BARBARA SHEPPARD has been sewing on and off for 30 years. She takes inspiration from vintage clothing and accessories and enjoys re-creating them into handbags. Her website, www.bsheppardstudio.com showcases her unique pieces. Recently, she's begun working with the owner of Kloset Kraze, a popular resale shop, to repurpose vintage neckties, scarves, and polyester fabrics into one-of-a-kind pieces under the name She-Su Designs. See more at shesu2008.etsy.com.

GIGI THORSEN has never met a bead or fabric she doesn't like, and her office/craft room is bursting with the proof. Just give her 10 minutes alone in there, and the craftiness begins! Gigi holds a degree in communications and is the founder of the Gold Ribbon—an international childhood cancer awareness symbol inspired by her daughter Kelsey. Her idea of non-crafting fun is playing golf, watching reality TV, and taking cruises. She has been married for 22 years and is the proud mother of three daughters. You can visit Gigi's online store at dizzlepop.etsy.com.

JENNIFER WALLIN may spend her days toiling away at a 9 to 5 job, but crafting is always on her mind. Once she gets home at night to join her husband, dog, and two cats in Long Beach, California, Jennifer tries to cram in a little crafting to to feed her creative side. She has participated in monthly craft-a-longs to create aprons, potholders, and purses. To see more of her work, visit thefeltmouse.blogspot.com.

LAURRAINE YUYAMA used to work as a custom picture framer, but found herself wanting to create her own art instead. She left the glasscutters and frames behind and now spends her days surrounded with beautiful fabrics, buttons, ribbons, and clay. She takes inspiration from Japanese craft books and the Internet crafting community. When she's not crafting, she spends time with her little girl and husband. Laurraine's work is sold internationally from her home-based studio in Vancouver, Canada, and through her online shop at patchworkpottery.com.

acknowledgments

Does your favorite stuff look snug as a bug now? There's a bunch of people to thank for that!

Thank you, thank you, thank you to the talented designers who share their passion for cozies with us in these pages. This pretty little book wouldn't exist without the lovely projects they stitched up.

Props to the team at Lark that helped pull this book together: editorial assistant Kathleen McCafferty; editorial interns Katie Henderson and Courtney Metz; photo stylist and art director Megan Kirby; and Jeff Hamilton, Bradley Norris, and intern Meagan Shirlen, who all kept the ball rolling during art production.

Jessica Boing and Nancy Wood are much appreciated for making sure all the I's got dotted and the T's, crossed. Grateful thanks to photographer Stewart O'Shields and his assistant Megan Cox for putting the projects in the spotlight; Megan Shirlen did a beautiful job modeling them. Thanks to Robin Gregory for cozying up to the task of laying out the book. Susan McBride's sweet illustrations are like the frosting on the cake.

index